TRAVELS WITH MAX:

How My Dog Unleashed My Life

Janet Bennett

Equinox Group Publishing

Travels with Max:
How My Dog Unleashed My Life

Published By
Equinox Group Publishing
A Division of The Equinox Group
September 2008

Cover and Book Design by Kelly Novak
KellDesign, LLC
www.kellynovak.com

ISBN 978-0-9819041-0-8

Printed in the United States of America

To Jenny and Will with love.

Wisdom Begins In Wonder.

Socrates

Contents

*Dogs are not our whole life
but they make our life whole.*

Rogar Caras

Dear Reader,

Welcome to our story. It is a true story of our life, and we hope that you find something in it that supports your life journey as well.

I adopted Max, my wonderful yellow Lab, in 2004, and he completely changed or "unleashed" my life. Because of him, I moved to a new town, learned to drive a 33 foot motorhome by myself, had a number of challenging adventures, and basically learned to face my fears and accept whatever came into my life with grace and gratitude.

He truly changed my life, and only for the better. Our journey together has taught me so many things, and has made my life so much richer and more peaceful. He took me from a place where I was struggling to understand who and what I was, to a place where I live my life from my heart.

Our journeys together also opened my mind and heart to an awareness of a power bigger than myself, which I have come to call divine consciousness. I have come to believe that every experience we have in life is designed to bring us closer to our own personal connection with the divine. Every experience—whether we perceive it as positive or negative— is still a teacher for us in this regard.

You can reach us most easily through our website at www.travelswithmax.com. We plan to continue to share photos and updates of our travels though the website, and hope that you will enjoy them.

We also hope that you will share with us your reactions to the book, and insights regarding your own personal journey. We are all traveling this road called life together, and it would be nice to support one another along the way.

In Peace and Gratitude,
Janet and Max

Kindness is the language which the deaf can hear and the blind can see.

Mark Twain

Introduction

Imagine for a moment a world in which everyone got along and we all lived our lives with kindness. We supported each other in bringing our unique gifts into the world, and we shared resources so that everyone had enough. The planet was honored and protected. We placed a high priority on caring for children, the elderly, and those unable to care for themselves. And we got up each morning with a song in our heart, and went to bed each night with a grateful prayer.

That is a world that is possible for us to create, and, in fact, many people are working to create it every day. And it is certainly a world in which I would like to live.

So how do we create and live in such a fashion?

While there are many policy changes that need to be made at the national and global level to create such a world, there is also something that we can all do as individuals: become more loving and peaceful people, and bring that love and peace to everyone and everything in our lives.

Achieving that level of inner peace is easier said than done for most people—at least it certainly has been for me. But it can be done, particularly if you have help along the way.

And the biggest source of help on my journey came in the form of a three-year old, 100-pound yellow Labrador Retriever—Max—that I was fortunate enough to adopt in May of 2004.

And he truly "unleashed" my life: adopting him required me to face so many fears and challenges that I otherwise would never have faced, and, those experiences truly changed my life, as you will see in our story.

A big part of that change in my life was also learning to listen to and trust my own inner wisdom—something I stubbornly resisted for a very long time. But facing big fears and big challenges in life does have an impact on a person whether we want it to or not.

I have since come to appreciate all that these experiences have taught me—and to thank Max for being the catalyst that brought so much change and awareness into my life.

In looking back, I also appreciate how he taught me to embrace change in my life—something that I also tended to resist. Learning to be receptive to change is very empowering; it allows you to soften to life and embrace whatever comes instead of getting tight and trying to resist it.

It also dramatically lowers the level of stress in your life. Stress comes from trying to control life when it really is beyond our control.

Peace comes when we give up that idea and embrace whatever life brings our way—and look for the lesson it is trying to bring to us. That is how we become loving and peaceful people: accepting life as it is.

And I will go one step further. I have also come to believe that we not only have the capability of accepting life as it comes, but to also "court" change in our lives by becoming open to being guided by a higher power, call it God or the divine universe or whatever.

That state of being is what I refer to as consciousness: allowing our lives to be guided through a connection with the divine. And that connection comes through our inner divine essence being in touch with the greater divine universe.

A divine connection from our hearts to our higher power.

I realize that some of this may be a little difficult for some people to accept, and that is fine. I certainly wasn't aware of any of it for most of my life. But somewhere along the line I began to ask some big questions like "why am I here?" or "who am I?" And I believe that those questions started me on a journey of personal discovery that led me to the point where I am now: a believer in divine consciousness and learning to allow it to lead my life.

And Max has been my greatest teacher, as you will see in our story. I may have given him the gift of freedom by running and playing "off leash," but he gave me a far greater gift of opening or "unleashing" my life to be all that it could possibly be.

So come, join Max and me—and everyone else in the story—as we travel on our life journey and see what we learn along the way.

Good luck on your own journey, and we hope you enjoy our story.

One can never consent to creep when one feels an impulse to soar.

Helen Keller

Part One

My knees were knocking. Big time. I never really knew what that expression meant until now. It apparently meant that your knees shake uncontrollably—as mine were at the moment. And with good reason since I had almost wiped out a burgundy van as I had tried to change lanes a moment ago.

Obviously, I had a blind spot in my passenger side mirror—which is no small problem when I'm driving a 33-foot motorhome by myself. Actually, I'm not alone, I have Max, my 100-pound yellow Lab with me, but he—as smart as he is—just hasn't gotten the knack for helping me drive this thing yet.

Neither had I. This was my first trip driving the motorhome—a 1992 Fleetwood Coronado—by myself. And while I had driven it with my friend, Bob, in the past, he had really managed the vehicle and I was just a second driver for short periods when he needed a break.

This, I was beginning to realize, was a whole different kettle of fish. And it was a little late to be realizing it since it was loaded for a month-long trip and I was currently trying to out-run a snowstorm that was bearing down on my hometown of Mentor, Ohio.

It was March 5, 2005, and we had just gotten a break in our winter weather that wasn't expected to last long. I had been waiting for just such an occasion to escape in the motorhome, and it looked like today was going to be the last good day for quite a while. And I was feeling pretty excited—even somewhat desperate—to get out of town and find some warm weather.

I had already prepared the motorhome for travel, but it was still in storage when I made the decision to leave. After calling the storage facility to make arrangements to get the motorhome out, I started packing as quickly as I could.

While you can prepare a motorhome for travel in advance, there is still a lot to be done the day you decide to leave, and it all seemed to take an endless amount of time that morning. It may have been because I was nervous about the whole thing and was having trouble concentrating on what I was doing.

Whatever the reason, I was finally done loading the car with the many bags of stuff that I somehow felt I couldn't live without as well as Max and all of his gear.

We headed over to the storage facility and loaded up the motorhome with all the bags from the car. I had made arrangements to leave my car in the storage facility while I was gone so I would have a ride home when I got back.

Finally, about 1 pm that afternoon, we were ready to hit the road. Max was on the big sofa behind the driver's seat wearing his safety harness, which would allow him room to move around on the sofa but also keep both of us safe.

He had been a good traveler for the short trips we had taken to get the motorhome serviced, but he had a tendency to want to come up and see what was happening out the front window.

That did not seem like such a good idea for a long trip since he could inadvertently knock into me while I was driving, and a 100-pound dog is no small bump. So for his safety and mine (and everyone else's on the road), I had brought his car safety harness along and he seemed content to stay on the sofa.

So off we went into the wild blue yonder. The weather was overcast as we pulled onto Rt. 2 that would take us to I-90 East and then on to the Outer Banks in North Carolina.

Our first destination was a visit to our friend, Maureen, who has a home there, and a week of sun and fun with her two black Labs.

But first we had to get there. And at the rate we were going, we wouldn't be getting very far very fast.

Two

Almost wiping out that burgundy van was unnerving to say the least. And I'm sure whoever blasted his horn at us in the van was a little unnerved as well.

So now what, I think to myself. What do I do now? I can't drive all the way to North Carolina with a big blind spot in my passenger side mirror.

I thought about turning around and going back to Mentor, but that seemed too awful to consider seriously. I had worked so hard to get ready for this trip— arrangements with neighbors, taking care of bills and banking matters, shopping for groceries, packing—endless packing and repacking—that I really didn't want to turn around and undo it all.

And the biggest reason was that I knew that I really needed to make this trip—fear and all—as part of my own personal journey.

So I discarded the idea of going back. Forward, I needed to go forward, but safely if I could figure out how to fix my mirror problem.

Motorhomes use large truck mirrors—they are designed to be able to let the driver see as well as possible the entire length of both sides of the motorhome. However, most of the time there are two people on board, and the passenger can look in that mirror to help the driver know if there are any vehicles in the blind spot.

But I didn't have anyone in the passenger seat at the moment. And, as I said earlier, Max—while a wonderful companion—wasn't much help with this problem.

Think, Janet, think. How can I fix this problem? And how can I fix it without losing a lot of time? I was worried about the weather and knew I needed to put some miles between me and the storm coming behind me.

Camping World! I could drive to Camping World and see if they could help me. It was a little out of my way but not too far—and I really needed a better mirror.

Two hours later and I'm back on the highway with a new mirror clamped onto my old one. It wasn't a perfect solution but an improvement. The service tech guys at Camping World had been nice enough to stop their work and to come out and see what they could do for me.

Of course, they loved Max and he loved them—Camping World is very dog friendly since a lot people who travel in recreational vehicles (RVs) bring their pets along.

The men suggested the mirror extension and adjusted both mirrors so I could see at least the majority of the passenger side of the motorhome.

So we were finally on the road again. We picked up the Ohio Turnpike that would take us southeast to Pennsylvania and on to the Outer Banks in North Carolina.

The Ohio Turnpike was a pretty well maintained road so I was beginning to feel a little more at ease as we drove along. But it was already almost 4 pm and starting to get a little dark—and we had only traveled about 50 miles.

So my mind starts in again with the "what are you doing?" Why are you trying to do this all by yourself?

Good question, I said to myself. I probably am nuts to be doing this, but it's too late to turn back now.

So why had I decided to take this trip? And by myself in a big motorhome?

The answer to that was Max and my love of traveling. I had always loved to drive and had been taking long driving quests over the last several years.

That type of travel was very soulful for me—it gave me a chance to go wherever I felt like going and I always found interesting people and places along the way. Since I made these drives alone, I had complete freedom to just trust my intuition and see where it led me.

And it was a way to practice giving up "control" over my life, or rather what I thought was control. But more on that later.

The other reason was Max. Max had come into my life in May of 2004. I had agreed to keep him for a few days while my friends, Maureen and Steve, helped to find a new home for him.

His former owners had decided they didn't want him anymore and had asked the place where he was being boarded to find him a new owner. My friends had heard about the dog and had offered to take him for a while so he wouldn't have to remain in a crate at the boarders.

And, as they say, the rest is history. Max came and stayed with me and never left. And so if I was going to make a driving quest this year, it was going to be with Max.

I had worked really hard over the last year to help him get over his separation anxiety and I wasn't about to leave him and have to start that process all over again. Besides, I had fallen in love with the big mutt and really didn't want to be apart from him.

Yes, I could have driven my car but that wasn't ideal either. First of all, it's hard to find motels that allow dogs, and if they do allow them, they have weight limits that don't usually include 100-pound dogs. And second, I really wanted to continue with my unplanned mode of travel and that would be difficult if not impossible given the motel problem.

So the motorhome seemed like the perfect solution. Max and I could go wherever we wanted and take our bed along with us.

Motorhomes are really a great way to travel: you have a miniature home on wheels and you don't have to drag suitcases into a motel every night. Yes, I only get about 10 miles to the gallon, but it comes out pretty even when you consider the money you save on meals, motel bills, and other car related travel expenses.

I loved to travel in the motorhome and thought that it would be a lot more comfortable for Max as well. I also wanted to do some writing on the trip and I have always felt more inspired in the motorhome for some reason. I felt that way from the very first time I stepped on board it in the spring of 1999—and I'm pretty sure I'll always feel that way.

So I really wanted to take the motorhome on the trip and it seemed like a good idea in theory. And I knew I'd be scared to do it on my own, but I didn't think I'd be this scared.

It is just so big. Motorhomes come in all shapes and sizes, but mine is 33 feet long—and that's big. It's built on a large truck chassis, and has a maximum weight of 16,000 pounds.

The scary part is turning it. It requires wide turns and you just have to learn where your back tires are to turn it correctly. That takes practice and I hadn't had much. It had been years since I had driven it at all, let alone by myself.

So I knew I would be afraid but that was part of the choice to take it as well. I had learned in other situations how beneficial it was for me to face my fears.

In my mind, *courage is feeling the fear and doing it anyway.* This belief had always rewarded me with a stronger sense of inner confidence and faith in myself—and faith in my angels as well.

This was all running through my mind as I'm driving down the highway, and I laughed to myself and concluded that I'd be one confident lady by the time I got home given how much fear I was feeling at the moment.

It also seemed like a good time to offer a quick prayer for extra guidance and protection during our little adventure.

And so our trip begins.

Three

We made it as far as Breezewood, Pennsylvania that first night. That was the last service plaza on the Pennsylvania Turnpike before we headed south.

I needed to stop somewhere that allowed RVs to park overnight and I wasn't sure what we'd find once we left the turnpike. The service plaza also provided 24 hour access to a restaurant and restrooms—which I needed since the motorhome was still winterized, which meant no running water.

We had made it there safe and sound but the driving had been tough. It had started to rain when it got dark and that made the driving all that much harder.

I really had wanted to put some miles behind me, but I've since learned that driving in the rain and the dark is not such a great idea. It's just too dangerous. You can't see the road clearly so you can't avoid the ruts and potholes—which is hard on both the motorhome and the passengers since you feel it much more than in a car.

You also can't see rocks in the road that could easily cause an accident. Nor can you see very far in front of you which means you might have difficulty stopping that big of a vehicle if you needed to in a hurry.

In hindsight, I was very foolish driving in those conditions—particularly as such an inexperienced driver. The Pennsylvania Turnpike was not in good condition at the time and would be a challenging drive through the Appalachian Mountains under the best of conditions, let alone in the dark with freezing rain falling.

It is one of the many occasions where I look back and just know that I must have been traveling under the protection of angels. And I'm sure that I kept several of them very busy that night.

Four

The next day we woke up very early—about 4 am—because it was so cold inside the motorhome. We didn't have any heat since I didn't know if I could use the propane furnace in such cold temperatures. It seemed wiser to be cold than to risk an explosion.

Anyway, it was cold enough to see my breath so I decided we might as well hit the road and head south towards warmer climate. I walked and fed Max and then made a quick dash to the washroom for myself.

It was still pitch black outside and a light frost was on the grass. This meant the road conditions were not ideal but, again, I didn't know that at the time. Anyway, after securing a few things that might fall while I was driving, I fired up the engine and off we roared.

One of the funny things that I noticed during those early days was the curious looks that people gave us. I'm sure they were surprised to see a small woman driving that big of a motorhome and being watched over by a very big dog looking out of the window right behind her.

It made me feel like we were an oddity—which we probably were and are—but I just smiled and waved and tried to look confident.

I'm not sure how convincing I was though since I also noticed that drivers coming towards us on single lane highways would often give me a wide berth when we were passing each other. But, again, that just made me laugh and say to myself that it was probably a good idea for them to give me extra space.

I should say that I have since become a very capable driver. It will never be easy for me to drive this big of a vehicle, but I'm no longer panic-stricken over it either. I've logged enough miles, backed up enough times, and gotten out of tight situations often enough to feel confident that I can manage it reasonably well.

But I never take it for granted; I drive slowly and mindfully always.

Five

So off we went on Day 2 of our trip, eager to get out of the cold Pennsylvania mountains and onto the warm sands of the Outer Banks.

But about an hour into our trip, a light snow began to fall.

Darn, I said to myself—or maybe something a little stronger.

I was smart enough to know that driving a motorhome in snow was not a great idea, but I was also now on a relatively isolated road with no good place to stop and park.

So I kept going.

That morning was another tiring drive in the dark and with the light snow falling. But eventually I could see daylight beginning to break and I began to feel a little better.

My co-pilot, Max, had been peacefully sleeping through the whole morning—making me wonder who was actually the wiser here. But he roused himself when he felt me braking.

That actually became a noticeable pattern—he would sleep soundly while I was driving but then would wake up quickly as soon as I started to put on the brakes. I guess he figured out that the change in motion signaled that something new was going to occur and he had better check it out.

That morning also set another pattern for us—pulling into the golden arches for a morning snack. I hadn't felt like eating before we left, so I was hungry and Max is always up for a meal.

I don't know if he is actually hungry or if he follows in the Lab tradition of always being eager for a meal, but he is always first in line for any type of experience involving food. And pretty much any type of food is fine with him.

His reaction pulling into McDonald's that first morning was relatively mild—he hadn't yet associated the sight of the golden arches to the egg mcmuffin with sausage and orange juice that would become our standard fare on these occasions.

But he is one smart dog—it only took one or two times and he began to know what was coming whenever I pulled into a McDonald's parking lot. He would give a couple of joyful barks to let me know that he was pleased by the decision.

I was just grateful to be off the road. I was still cold and feeling pretty tired after all that we had been through so far.

My 55th birthday was only weeks away and my body was feeling the affects of sitting in a cold motorhome, rattling down the highway for hours on end. So I was very grateful for the warmth of the restaurant, the access to a rest room, and, of course, the food.

That little breakfast—shared with my buddy Max and eaten at our own table in the motorhome—marked the first of many experiences of almost complete peace.

I felt such a wonderful feeling of contentment as we watched the sun come fully into being and shower us with its beautiful white light. Yes, I had been naïve about what was really involved with such an undertaking, but it was becoming a wonderful adventure.

Gone were the aches and pains, replaced by little bubbles of joy that I just couldn't contain.

And that marked the nature of our trip: trials and tribulations every step of the way, balanced by moments of awe-inspiring contentment and joy.

Six

I had known before beginning the trip that it was what I needed to do in order to break free from some negative life habits: like eating and drinking too much, and wasting too much time in front of the TV.

I had been on a journey of personal discovery for a long time—over a decade—and had made a lot of progress along the way. But then I got stuck. Stuck in a rut of living what I've come to know as the "small version" of my life.

I could envision the big version: living my life with grace and using all the talents that God had given me. But I couldn't get there.

The blockages were too strong: fear of what that "path" would bring, fear about how I'd make a living, worry about what my family and friends would think, and a general question of whether I was nuts to even be thinking this way.

I've come to believe that we are all on our own personal journeys—not just to survive in this life, but to really come to know who we uniquely are, and to live fully in that wisdom. Now that would be a life well-lived.

But there are so many things that seem to be working against that realization, and I have to admit that my own journey has been marked by some very powerful forces of resistance to that new reality.

At the time of this first RV trip with Max, I was struggling—and losing—to those forces of resistance. And that is what the trip turned out to be—a big reckoning with those forces—me, Max and the divine universe against all the old wounds, fears, and other baggage that were holding me back.

And it worked—not completely—it took more trips and more challenges to push me further down my path, but it certainly was a big boost forward.

And I hope by sharing these adventures—with all their highs and lows—that it might inspire someone else to begin to see their own life as their own special story: we are all beautiful, unique, divinely inspired creatures. We just have to break through our "disguises" to fully see and celebrate the unique beings we all are.

So let our journey of "disguise shedding" begin.

Seven

After getting fortified by food, sunshine and good feelings, we once again headed the motorhome south—being drawn by the vision of sand, surf and good company.

The goal for the first leg of our trip was to get to Avon—a small city in the Outer Banks of North Carolina—where our friend Maureen lived in the winter with her two black Labs, Rhymer and Seager.

As mentioned earlier, Maureen and Steve had "rescued" Max back in May of 2004, and were the ones who had brought him into my life.

It is common for dogs in Max's situation—given up or abandoned by their former owners—to be referred to as rescue dogs because we see them as being rescued from these unfortunate living situations.

In Max's case, it probably was his size that made his first home situation difficult. People often don't fully know or appreciate what a big dog requires until it's too late. That cute puppy turns into a big beast if it's not properly trained.

Which just reminds us that it's very important to do your homework before you bring that cute puppy home: know what you're getting into for everyone's sake.

For whatever reason, Max's former owners hadn't trained or regularly exercised him, and had left him in a crate most of the time. So I had inherited a very large, undisciplined, and out-of-shape three year-old dog.

In looking back at that time, I really cannot say why I knew that I had to put a high priority into training him. I would have to say that I was "guided" in that direction since I really had no prior knowledge of what a challenge a 100-pound dog could be once he got some muscle strength in his legs.

I have since come to learn that big, strong dogs can do whatever they want to do—at least when up against a middle-aged, small woman—unless they are properly trained.

So I am very fortunate that I was led to begin training him right away and that we made such fast progress. Max passed the American Kennel Club's (AKC) Canine Good Citizen test about six months after I adopted him, and he passed the Therapy Dogs International (TDI) test about three months after that. Max has such a lovable personality that I just knew that he would be a great dog for pet therapy work.

I would probably not have been able to keep Max without this commitment to a lot of training. All dogs, and obviously big ones in particular, require a lot of exercise, and without it they can become very unhappy and even unruly.

Knowing this, I also knew that there was no way that I was going to be able to give Max the amount of exercise he needed without him being able to run off leash. Long walks are fine, but a good run is even better. Being a Labrador Retriever, he naturally loved to chase and retrieve balls, frisbees, etc., and he was able to do so once he was trained to be off-leash.

And while I was out exercising Max, I was also exercising myself—which I desperately needed.

Part of my being "stuck" was a lack of energy to be physically active—which I had always been in the past and was missing terribly. So by my giving time and attention to Max's physical care, I was also giving it to myself.

So, once again, I have came to appreciate this guidance, and firmly believe that dogs—and pets in general—often come into our lives at exactly the right time to help us along on our journeys.

So it's probably more appropriate to say that Max rescued me and not the other way around—or that the universe brought us together to rescue—really heal—each other.

And that has certainly been the case during the time that Max has been in my life. There have been, and continue to be, so many experiences with Max that have taught me so much and made such a big contribution to my personal growth—as well as bringing a great deal of fun and joy into my life.

I would even go so far as to say that Max has been a guiding angel in my life: adopting him has significantly influenced the course of my life, and as far as I can tell, only for the better.

But no matter what we call our pets, we can certainly appreciate them for the great gifts of unconditional love and acceptance that they bring into our lives.

Eight

Maureen and Steve also have two wonderful angels in their lives: Rhymer and Seager. Both are black Labrador Retrievers and are about a year younger than Max. The three dogs always have a grand time together, and I was looking forward to several days of fun with the dogs on the beach.

But we had to get there first, and nature was once again throwing us a challenge: more snow.

Not just the light snow we had traveled in earlier, but an honest to goodness snowstorm—in March in Virginia. We made it to Norfolk, Virginia before it started coming down in earnest and forced us to stop.

We parked at the local Wal-Mart—the store allows RVers to park there for as long as necessary, including overnight. We had found a parking spot away from the main parking area so we wouldn't get boxed in and not be able to leave.

Parking lots across America are built for cars, not RVs, so you need a big lot in order to take the two spaces necessary for the length of most motorhomes, and have enough room to make the turns to get out of the lot.

So we sat and watched and waited as this snowing thunderstorm went barreling through the area.

Common sense had told me to park on the side of the building that might offer the best protection from the storm—which we did—but we were still getting rocked pretty strongly from the force of the winds.

Not a real comfortable feeling.

But, after a couple of hours, the storm blew through, the sun came out, and we started to feel a lot better.

Not that great peace and contentment I had felt from the morning "sun show", but relieved and happy to be in one piece just the same.

Only now there was about two good inches of snow everywhere and we see no sign of anyone doing anything about it—like plowing the roads.

We are far enough south by this point that snow plows,

etc., are a lot less plentiful than up north, so I figure the snow is just going to be there for awhile.

So now that we are marooned in the Wal-Mart parking lot, what was a girl to do?

Shop of course. So after I give Max a quick walk, it's off to shop for a few supplies that we need. Since motorhomes have limited storage capacity, there isn't a lot that I can stock up on so the shopping trip doesn't take very long.

By now it's after 3 pm and, while the southern sun shining on me as I walked back to the motorhome was surprising strong, the snow was still on most of the parking lot and the roads looked pretty slushy.

I had talked to a few people in the store about the likelihood of the roads getting cleared anytime soon, and they weren't very optimistic. They called it a freak storm that caught everyone by surprise.

More importantly, they also told me that the high winds had probably closed several bridges to tall vehicles, including the one that I needed to cross to continue our journey, so going anywhere further was unlikely.

I was also beginning to feel the affects of the traveling we had already done, and a meal and warm bed were starting to sound very good indeed.

The meal part I had taken care of in the store—but the warm bed was another matter. A warm anything required electricity since using propane as a source of energy was not yet an option given my lack of knowledge and experience about how that system worked.

So I called Maureen to give her an update on our progress—only to learn that the bridges in her area were also closed to tall vehicles due to the storm.

But no problem—we'd just camp around there for the night. Again, traveling in a motorhome is great because you have everything you need right at hand.

We could stay in the Wal-Mart parking lot and "dry camp" (no electric, water or sewer hookups) or try and find an RV campground in the area.

With the help of our trusty Woodall's Campground Directory—which listed every state park and public RV campground in the country—we found a campground about five miles away that we could stay at for the night.

So on March 6, 2005, Max and I stayed in our very first RV campground together.

I want to mark that date because at that point I wasn't sure if it was also going to be our last campground experience.

Between the very challenging two days of driving and the appearance of this hole-in-the-wall campground, I was beginning to have serious doubts about the whole trip.

Because of the storm, the campground probably did not present itself at its best—the roads were wet and muddy, there was a fair amount of debris around, and it seemed almost deserted—in a very eerily way.

And once again, that old "voice of reason" in my head began to do its number on me: is it safe to stay here? Will we be attacked out here in the middle of nowhere? How can I defend us if some beer-drinking buddies decided to pay us a visit?

But of course we were fine. I hadn't stayed in that many RV campgrounds and I must have been expecting something a little nicer.

But it was perfectly safe and the owners were very pleasant

and accommodating to "the little lady with the great big dog" as the owner was fond of saying. I had taken Max in with me to register as a little extra protection—not that he would ever hurt anyone, but his size can be intimidating.

Of course, one big dog biscuit from the campground owner and Max was all wags and kisses. And a couple of guys sitting on the porch gave him several good pats or really thumpings that had him circling around them like a cat begging for more.

So much for my great protector.

I write about this experience almost exactly three years— and many RV campgrounds—later, and I have to laugh at myself and my suburban way of seeing life at that time. I can honestly say that I have never had a bad experience in any of the campgrounds that we have stayed at—little or big—and have enjoyed every one of them.

The people in this business are some of the nicest people I have ever had the privilege to meet. They normally are very genuine and generally take great pride in their campgrounds.

The campgrounds we stay at are all rated and regularly inspected by the Woodall's team, and the description of the amenities of the campgrounds are generally pretty accurate so you can know what to expect. We also joined the Good Sam Club and KOA, and use those directories and parks frequently as well.

So in the three-years that we've been traveling in the motorhome, we have had some wonderful experiences, and I am now a great deal more confident than I felt on that first snowy night in Virginia.

Nine

So we survived to continue on our journey the next day. The sun was out and rapidly drying up the puddles in the campground as I took Max out for his walk before we departed.

I had only plugged in the main power cord the evening before—so we could have electricity in the coach—so I didn't have much to do to prepare for our departure.

Motorhomes come equipped with all the basic systems of a house—water, sewer, and three sources of power: 1) a main electrical cord for 30 or 50 amps of power that run the main electrical system, including the microwave, air conditioners, TV, etc.; 2) a propane tank that runs the furnace, hot water heater, refrigerator and stove; and, 3) a generator for emergencies when other electrical power is not available.

When you are in an RV park, full hook-ups (electric, water and sewer) are normally available so you can use all your systems with ease. That really makes the RV experience the most pleasant but you can also learn to live with less.

On that first night in Virginia, I decided to only plug in the main electrical cord so we could have all the electricity we needed. That would allow me to use my electric heating pad on the bed and make a nice cup of tea on my little electric burner in the morning, as well as be able to use all the other electrical appliances in the coach.

I didn't hook up the water lines because the motorhome was still winterized (antifreeze in the lines) and I wanted to leave it that way until we were well beyond any risk of a freeze at night.

And I hadn't used the bathroom for the same reason so there was no need to hook up the sewer lines either.

All of which was a good thing since I had only a vague recollection of how to do all that at the time. My earlier trips in the motorhome had been with Bob who took care of all of that for us.

My job was to bring him coffee and danish while he was driving, cook our meals, and keep things organized on the inside. We had an "inside-outside" division of chores so to speak, so my experience with all the outside hook-ups was pretty limited to say the least.

In fact, some of the most embarrassing moments of my life were when we arrived at several campgrounds late in the afternoon—after most everyone else had set up for the night—and I had to go out and set up the lines by myself.

Not only was I an oddity traveling without a man, but I also clearly didn't really know what I was doing. And I'm sure I provided a lot of amusement to several families as they sat around their campfires and watched the "poor woman traveling alone" try and get her lines hooked up.

Well, I'm happy to report that I'm now a "pro" at the whole thing so I'm no longer going around embarrassing my gender. I also learned not to be the last to arrive at the campground so it took some of the pressure off of me as I was learning how to do all that.

But it also taught me that we are really a society of couples: I was almost always the only woman traveling by herself and people really did find that odd. And it took me quite a while not to feel odd about it myself.

I'll never forget the sweet woman who came rushing over one afternoon as I was going about the setting up process and asked me if she should send her husband over to help me. She had been watching us and hadn't seen my husband come out and wondered if he was inside and sick or something, and therefore, maybe I needed a hand.

When I explained to her that I was traveling alone with my dog, she about fainted. She literally had to sit down at the picnic table and catch her breath. I'm pretty sure I've never seen anyone's eyes get that wide that fast before.

But we ended up having a great laugh over it and she walked away shaking her head over the "strange woman from up north."

Before we left the next day, she asked if she could take a picture of me and Max for her family back home who just would never believe her story about us without proof. So somewhere out there is a picture or two of Max and me in someone's scrapbook—hopefully without the caption "crazy lady and her dog" under the picture.

I should mention that I've since learned that there are actually a lot of women who travel by themselves in motorhomes. Many travel in groups and there are several support organizations that plan trips and provide other services.

In addition, many wives help with the driving, and it's always a good idea to know how to do it in case of an emergency if the husband is injured or can't drive for some reason.

While I'm sure that we were and still are a novelty for a lot of the people we meet on our travels, I really feel that Max and I have left behind a long trail of people who have a much greater appreciation for what women (and dogs) can do if they put their minds to it.

I've also noticed that there seems to be a lot higher level of acceptance in the campgrounds that we visit now that I know what I'm doing—experience does pay off.

Ten

OK, so back to Day 3 of our journey.

The weary and still wet-behind-the-ears travelers are once again back on the road and heading south to the Outer Banks. And this time we got there. Not without incident, but we did arrive at Maureen's house later that afternoon.

As we left Norfolk, we continued on I-64 East that would take us on to North Carolina. We exited at Nags Head, and it brought back memories of a driving quest that I had taken in the spring of 2002.

That was my first driving quest and I was on a "go wherever the wind blows me" path, and it blew me to Nags Head. I had decided to get off the freeway at that exit because it made me laugh, and made me think that my kids would find that a very fitting choice since I was such a nag about their homework, etc. as they were growing up. I also love horses so I thought that was the place for me.

I took what I have come to call driving quests every spring in 2002, 2003, and 2004 for many of the same reasons that I was taking the one in the motorhome in 2005—to break out of the box that I felt I had built around myself in the first fifty-some years of my life.

And the quests always worked. I always came back feeling like I knew myself better, and that I had been able to release some old grudges and heal some old wounds—of which I seemed to have quite a supply.

I suppose no one goes through life without being wounded in some way, shape or form—and most people probably experience a fair amount of it.

I was raised in the generation of "be nice and don't say anything bad"—which included any negative emotion such

23

as anger, disagreement, etc. Accordingly, I had repressed lot of negative emotional energy.

I say had here because I've "excavated" a lot of it over the last several years—not all but probably most of it by this point. I know this because I no longer have the same emotional "charge" around old experiences like I use to.

Now, in fact, I see everything that I've experienced in life as a gift to teach me something important about myself— so I feel more appreciation for the experiences than I do hurt or anger.

But I'm getting ahead of myself. I hadn't gotten to this emotional point by our RV adventure in 2005, which is one reason why I needed to take it.

But it's clear that traveling on my own was for me—and still is—a very healing thing for me to do. It really forced me to see myself more clearly—who else was there?—and face the fears that were so powerfully holding me in an old, stuck, and fairly negative pattern.

This story reflects my experiences about midway in that journey and how they helped lead me to the place where I am today.

Eleven

Back to the trip. After we took the exit off I-64, we headed south until we reached Nags Head where we stopped for lunch.

It brought back a lot of memories and made me realize how much I had changed since my visit there in 2002.

During that first quest, I was very anxious about what I was doing, and filled with a lot of fear. I was also very concerned about what other people thought of my trip, and really didn't feel comfortable telling people that I was "just out driving around the country."

I knew it was what I needed to do; I just couldn't say it. I was afraid that they would think that I was crazy, which would have undermined my commitment to my path— probably enough to throw me off it. So I just kept it to myself.

But sitting in the motorhome three years later was a very different story.

I was proud of myself for having the courage to stick to my path—no matter how outside the mainstream of society it seemed—and I was pleased with the personal freedom that it had brought me.

After all, there I was in a 33-foot motorhome and driving it by myself. And I had actually met several challenges pretty well along the way.

I also realized that I had gotten quite a way past the need to organize my life to please other people—or to let my fear of "what they might think" run my life.

Which was actually saying quite a lot in my case.

Many years earlier I had begun to recognize how much the opinion of others mattered to me, and how that "need to please" had affected my life.

 I use to laugh about it (actually laughed and cried in equal measure), and would tell myself that someone should just stamp a capital P right in the middle of my forehead and make me President of the People Pleasers Club.

Over the course of my personal journey, I have come to understand just how big a barrier the need to please others really has been in my life.

And I suspect in many other people's lives as well.

So sitting in the motorhome in Nags Head three years later, I could feel the difference in myself—the growth that had taken place. I wasn't completely free of that need to please issue, but it had a lot less power over me. I had reclaimed enough of myself that I could actually handle it if I displeased other people with the choices I made in my life.

I knew I wasn't completely done with it because a few people still had some power over me, but I had come a long way. And I knew at that point that there was no going back—I would never give my power away like that again.

So I said a prayer of gratitude for my progress and fired up the motorhome for the last leg of our trip to Maureen's. And said several prayers as we drove over some very tall bridges as we left Nag's Head—the winds were still pretty strong and were blowing the motorhome around a bit. I just tried to keep it steady and didn't look down at the water.

Twelve

Except for the drive over the bridges, the rest of the way there was pretty smooth since the sun had come out and the roads were dry.

It was at that point that I began to realize how much easier and safer it is to drive a motorhome in the daylight and on dry roads. And I realized that I had been driving it like a car, not a motorhome.

Those first two days of driving—through the rain, mountains, and snow—had been incredibly challenging and tiring. Day three was a breeze by comparison. I was actually enjoying chugging on down the highway and feeling far more confident of my driving.

Right then and there I decided I would never again drive in the dark, heavy rain or other unsafe conditions, and I haven't. Now I am on the road after daybreak and off it by 3 or 4 pm in the afternoon.

With a stop at midmorning and one for lunch, it gives both me and Max just the right mix of traveling and rest time. And I always take the time for him to have a nice walk and some playtime when we stop.

So we finally pulled into Maureen's driveway about 3 pm that afternoon. Steve, unfortunately, was not there because he had work to do in Cleveland. But Maureen, Rhymer and Seager were spending a couple of months of the winter in the Outer Banks.

We were greeted by the joyful barking of Rhymer and Seager once they saw Max—or rather heard him. Maureen and I had talked before hand and had agreed that we would take the three dogs on a walk as soon as we got there to help them discharge all their extra energy and let them chase each other somewhere other than inside the house.

So we had a nice walk on the beach and the dogs had a good time fetching balls, running in the waves and chasing each other in circles. When we were all thoroughly worn out, we walked home while enjoying a beautiful sunset.

I was so glad to be exactly where I was at that moment— and so glad not to be back up north in the cold and snow.

Walking on the beach with my good friend and three beautiful and joyful dogs made all the work of getting there worth it. And, I must confess, I was very pleased with the idea that I was not going to have to drive the motorhome again for a whole week.

Thirteen

We had a great time with Maureen, Rhymer and Seager for the next week. Maureen and I fixed a lot of great meals, drank some good wine, and talked and talked and talked.

Her daughter Tracey and her two daughters, Grace and Anna, joined us during the week. Tracey even gave me a great and much needed haircut. Her husband John and son Jack had remained in Cleveland. Steve has two daughters, Kristin and Michelle, and Michelle was enjoying a visit to the beach as well.

So we had a house full of kids, dogs, sunshine and laughter.

Maureen is a great friend and confidant, and we have been exploring similar personal and spiritual issues for many years.

I have also been blessed with several other women friends who have been a part of my life for a very long time— some for over thirty years. We raised our children together and supported each other every step of the way. We now call ourselves the Daleford Dames from the street we all lived on—and Beth, Chris, Flo and Sandi and I still get together on a regular basis to share the events of our lives. These are friendships that I will treasure always.

At some point in my life, my personal journey began to include a very compelling interest to explore the big questions in life: who am I really? What is my true purpose in life? What values do I really want to live by?

And I have found it very helpful to explore these questions with friends who are also reading, studying and generally trying to figure them out as well. And the beach is such an awe-inspiring place to be that it made it even nicer when Maureen and I would go for long "walk and talk" sessions with the dogs.

And Max, Rhymer and Seager had a great time together too. The dogs are great pals, and it is always a lot of fun to watch them play together. It is also a relief that they get along so well since they were all big dogs and all males to boot.

But they got along fine that week, and were really cute with each other. When they were done with their playtime, all three of them would squeeze themselves together up on the sofa. They reminded us of an Oreo cookie with the two black labs on either end and the almost white lab in the middle.

All in all, it was a very memorable time.

Fourteen

I had been planning on staying at Maureen's for about a week before I would resume my open journey to parts unknown.

I was hoping to find a good place (preferably near the beach) where I could review the journals I had been writing for many years. I felt it would be helpful to review the journals and jot down some of the key insights and ideas that I had "received" during the journaling process.

I had started journaling many years earlier as a way to help me explore some of those big life questions. And also to help me sort out how I was feeling about my life and what I wanted to do about it. It served as a form of personal therapy I suppose—and still does.

The interesting thing is that—over time—I have been able to tap more and more into what I have come to see as my inner wisdom. Call it intuition, the inner voice, or even divine guidance—it always gave me helpful insights into the situation that life was presenting to me.

It was also a way for me to address the inner pain that

I was experiencing as I struggled to resolve old painful experiences in my life. And it was particularly helpful to me in dealing with the pain I was experiencing in a marriage that wasn't working, and which eventually lead to a divorce in 1993, after twenty years and two wonderful children later.

So my idea was to pick a nice warm spot near a beach and camp out in the motorhome with Max for a week or so and read through all those journals. And maybe write something from them as well, if sharing any of those insights would be of help to anyone else.

Even though it was mid-March, the weather in the Outer Banks had been on the cool side and pretty windy at times. Knowing that I was going to have to cross back over those tall bridges, I was watching the weather pretty closely so we could pick a good day to leave and begin our travels further south.

Fifteen

We found that day on March 14th. The sun was out, the winds were low, and it was time to say goodbye and hit the road again.

I felt a little more comfortable behind the wheel this time out. Maybe it was the rest I had gotten that past week. Whatever the reason, I felt eager to be off on the next leg of our journey.

I had intentionally not made any reservations at any campgrounds along the way since I really didn't want to travel on a charted route. It felt a lot more exciting to just follow our instincts and stop wherever and whenever we wanted.

And that proved to be a good choice.

I had been in something of a rush to get to Maureen's— both to out run the weather and also because she was expecting us since I had told her I thought I could get there in a couple of days of travel. And that may be reasonable time if traveling by car, but not necessarily for a motorhome—as we had recently learned.

But I had yet to learn how to travel in a relaxed way so that one could actually enjoy the trip. Max was to teach me how to do that on that very day.

Because the weather was cool when we left the Outer Banks, I once again got into my "must travel many miles by darkness" mindset in the hope of finding warmer weather.

After four long hours of driving that morning, I finally pulled into a rest stop for a bite to eat and to just take a break from driving.

Max seemed very happy to stop too, and I learned just how unhappy he had been during the long morning drive when he refused to get back in the motorhome after a very quick walk. He just plunked his rear down when I tried to hustle him back on board—and there's not a lot you can do to move a 100-pound dog when he doesn't want to move.

My first reaction was irritation at the delay, and I tried to command him to get in—nothing doing. Then I tried to bribe him with dog cookies—and surprise of surprises since he loves his dog treats—he still refused.

So it finally dawned on me that maybe he was sick and tired of traveling, and why was I in such a hurry anyway? Wasn't the point of the trip just to explore this part of the country with no particular agenda in mind?

So I quit trying to muscle him into the motorhome,

locked the door, and took him on a long walk around the rest area where we had stopped. And, of course, he went right in when we got back to the motorhome.

That is just another example of how Max has influenced my life—for the better. I had been mindlessly rushing around until then—really just out of habit I guess. "I must drive further and faster and not stop until I dropped" was apparently my unconscious mindset.

And that day Max showed me a much better way to travel, and really a much better way to live.

Sixteen

So we made our way—in a leisurely manner—southward, stopping for a short visit with another friend, Joan, in North Carolina before continuing on our way.

I wasn't sure where we were heading other than south to get into warmer weather. I had taken my kids for several years to Myrtle Beach, South Carolina during their school spring breaks, and had always loved the big white beaches there.

So I thought that would be a good place to head and to check out the RV campgrounds in that area. I had always had a picture in my mind of me sitting in the motorhome and writing—ideally near the beach.

As I mentioned before, I have always found the ocean to be so healing and inspiring. It has always drawn me, and all of my earlier quests had included some time being spent near the shore.

And then we got lucky when we got to Myrtle Beach. We found a lovely RV campground, and, better yet, they gave us an end site so we were able to park right next to the beach.

I say lucky but I don't really believe that it was luck. I believe it was divine intention or maybe the law of attraction. I had actually envisioned being there when I had driven through that very campground on one of my earlier quests, and had thought how great it would be to be camped there someday in the motorhome.

But I didn't realize the connection at the time.

When we had originally pulled into the campground to check it out, the sign had said no vacancy. But I thought I might as well pick up a brochure, and that is when I realized I had seen that brochure before and had been in that campground before.

So Max and I went over to talk to the manager to see if they might have an opening coming up anytime soon, and she told me that they were booked a year in advance. They were one of the most popular campgrounds in the area and were almost always full, particularly during that time of year.

So as we are chatting, the phone rings and the other office manager takes a message that a woman was canceling their reservation because her husband wasn't feeling well enough to drive.

So we got to stay after all—and then the office manager did us another favor by assigning us a large site at the end of the row so we could be right near the beach. "So you can walk that beautiful dog of yours more easily," she said.

At that time, I was pleasantly surprised by this fortunate turn of events, and grateful that we could get off the road and settled in a nice spot. But while I was surprised, I wasn't completely surprised because I had been having similar experiences over the years. And if you get enough of those kinds of experiences, you begin to wonder if they are surprises at all.

I now believe that the universe is one big field of energy and that you can tap into it if you truly believe in it. It is along the lines of that saying that the universe will bring you exactly what you need when you need it. That doesn't mean that it will bring you everything you want or think that you need, however. The divine universe is wiser than we are.

I believe that there is a greater divine wisdom in operation and that wisdom knows a lot more about what we really need than we do. At this point, I try to just trust it—actually surrender to it—and let it take me where it will.

That is what I have come to call faith, and it has taken me a very long time to understand what that really means and even more time to make a commitment to try and live my life that way.

But that was what this journey and more recent journeys were to teach me.

Seventeen

As mentioned earlier, I also believe that pets can be great teachers for us if we are only open to them. I absolutely know that Max has been and continues to be a great teacher in my life—really a guiding angel.

Before Max came into my life, I was very stuck and struggling to find my way. I will spare you the gory details, but suffice it to say that I was not doing so well on a personal level. While I was doing OK professionally, it still was an effort to get dressed and go to work every day, and I was exhausted by the time I got home.

I had downsized from a big house after my children were grown, and I had moved into a nice apartment complex that allowed dogs. This was important since my son, Will, who was still in college, had a dog, Mussie, and I wanted to have a place where they could come and stay.

And while the apartment was nice, I just felt like I was living in a dark tunnel. Some might call it depression, but it really felt like what I have come to understand as the "dark night of the soul."

I was clearly in the throes of a serious emotional cleansing, and I felt completely lost in the process. Like I knew I was in a dark tunnel and could see some light ahead every once in a while, but I couldn't find my out and into the daylight.

Now I see it more like when you clean out a very messy closet—you have to take everything out and make a big mess of it before you can organize and put things back in neatly. And a key factor in that cleaning process is to discard what you no longer need.

Max entered my life when everything was out of the closet and in a big mess on the floor. I could see and feel the mess, but I didn't have the energy or clarity to know how to put it back together. I didn't know it at the time, but Max was going to show me the way to do it.

Having Max in my life has made that process possible and I am pretty close to having a pretty tidy closet of a life— not perfect, but I no longer expect or even need perfection in my life.

Just contentment and peace.

Eighteen

Actually, I wasn't entirely surprised when Max came into my life.

I had been given several clues in prior years, and had even journaled about how great it would be to have a dog again.

I had to put our family dog, Tawny, down about four years earlier due to age and health issues, and it had broken my heart. I've always loved dogs, but I just couldn't bring myself to open my heart to another one quite yet.

But obviously the universe was getting tired of my procrastination. They had tried to get through to me before—including having a dog bed fall on my head in a store in 2002. And I bought it at the time—and it became Max's first dog bed two years later.

There was also the dog bowl that I bought on my quest in 2003 when I was in Asheville, North Carolina on my birthday. I just "had to have that pottery dog bowl" so I bought it as a birthday present to myself—and it became Max's first water bowl a year later.

Then, the final clue—that I completely missed until much later—was a picture of a dog on a car blanket that I tore out of one of those merchandise magazines on an airplane trip in the fall of 2003. I thought the dog blanket might be a good holiday gift for my son and his dog.

I really didn't look carefully at the dog, but I found that advertisement about six months after I adopted Max, and it looked exactly like him. I was absolutely astounded at the coincidence, and I still have the ad today just to remind myself of how the universe works. And there are no coincidences—these signs are all trying to tell us something.

I had also talked with several friends about getting a dog, including Maureen and Steve, but just hadn't done anything about it. Living in an apartment did not seem like the ideal situation for a dog so I had thought that I would just wait until I was in a house again.

So when Maureen called to ask if I could take care of a dog for a few days, I thought the universe might be at work again—only this time it had taken matters into its own hands.

And that is what I believe did happen, although I had my doubts when I first saw him.

Max had been staying at Harry's, who was Maureen's daughter Taryn's then boyfriend and now husband. They were interested in keeping him themselves but they both worked and weren't yet settled in the same house.

When we arrived, I thought Max looked like a big slightly yellow marshmallow. But I had agreed to take him for the weekend so that was that. Harry had to practically pick him up and put in the back of Maureen's car—he couldn't jump in by himself because he didn't have enough strength in his hindquarters.

So even though I believed that the universe had brought this dog to me for a reason, I wasn't initially thrilled by him. But something was telling me to look beyond what I was seeing at the moment and just open my heart to him.

But there were other factors that were making the decision to adopt him difficult as well.

As I said earlier, I was living in an apartment and that was clearly not a great set-up for such a big dog. Also, the apartment management wouldn't let me keep him on a permanent basis because they had a 25-pound weight limit for dogs.

So that meant that I would have to move, and I hated that idea. It had been very emotionally traumatic for me in the three moves that I had made in recent years, and I really didn't feel like I had the energy or emotional fortitude to do it again (remember I was in the "mess on the floor" stage of the closet analogy).

Also, it was clear that this dog was going to require a lot of time, energy and probably money. He wasn't trained in any way, and he had a bad case of separation anxiety, which he demonstrated by barking loudly whenever I tried to leave the apartment.

He also had several physical issues, including being about twenty pounds over-weight, and, since he had no muscles in his hindquarters, he just collapsed whenever he sat down.

My neighbor below me complained to the apartment manager—which I don't blame him for—because it sounded like I was dropping bowling balls up there every time Max sat down.

Plus the boarder had taken him to a vet because he was drinking so much water when he was in her care, and she thought he might be diabetic. He wasn't, but the vet did find that he had a twisted spine from being in too small of a crate for too many hours a day.

So I had some real reservations about the whole deal.

Max had been with me for only three or four days when Maureen called back to say that someone else was interested in adopting him, and they wanted Steve to bring him back to the boarding facility.

Labrador Retrievers are very popular dogs, and we suspected that the other person would adopt him if we took him back out there. So I had to make a decision and I had to make it quickly.

And, even with all the logical reservations running through my head, I just couldn't stand the idea of giving him up. It had only been a short while, but that was apparently all it took for him to work his way into my heart.

It was probably for the best that the decision had to be made that quickly or I might have over thought it, and may have made the mistake of giving him back.

So I told Maureen that I wanted to adopt him, and she and Steve managed to convince the owner of the boarding facility that I would give him a good home. The fact that I was in an apartment wasn't going over very well, but then they explained that I was going to have to move to keep him anyway.

Maureen's son, Torrey, who was studying to be a veterinarian at the time, helped Steve prepare the transfer of ownership papers, and within a week of getting the first call from Maureen, I had a new dog.

And a new life—I just didn't know it at the time.

Nineteen

The most immediate challenge was to find a new place to live. And that was proving to be a major problem.

I went online to search all the classified ads in local papers around the area to find an apartment or small house that would allow such a big dog. I had decided that I needed to continue to rent just because of the time constraints: I had to be out of the apartment I was in within a month if not sooner.

They really didn't want to allow me to keep Max there at all after my neighbor complained, but I just knew it wouldn't be good for us to be separated so soon. So I stalled them as best I could, but I needed to move and move quickly.

I must have called over 200 different apartment complexes and rental agents trying to find anyone who would allow such a big dog. The apartment complexes that did allow bigger dogs had a 75-pound weight limit and required a vet's certificate to prove it.

I couldn't believe how hard this search was getting to be, and it was getting more and more stressful with the clock ticking louder every day.

I also looked at a couple of houses to rent, but they didn't seem to fit the situation either. I was thinking that this move would be short-term and that I would probably buy a house in a year or so anyway.

Renting a house was also expensive and came with all the maintenance obligations. And it would be difficult to leave in the winter (pipes freezing, etc.) if I wanted to continue to travel—which is why I had sold my house three years ago in the first place.

While renting a house had the advantage of a yard for Max, which was very appealing, something in me told me not to go that route. And, as it has turned out, that was also good guidance since we clearly have needed to be free to continue our travels.

I finally found two condos that were possibilities. Two out of over 200. I was able to convince the owners that Max was a great dog and I had stopped telling them how much he weighed. I just said he was a loving Lab and wouldn't cause any problems.

The first place we looked at—I had to take Max with me because of the barking issue—was a dump, and I began to really worry that I was going to have to give him up after all.

Fortunately, the second place was small but quite nice, and I guess Max did a good job of charming the owners, Joanne Sadar and Jim Blackstone, because they agreed to rent us the condo.

Once I had the keys, I felt a great sense of relief. I'm not sure what I would have done if they hadn't been willing to take a chance on us. I just feel very grateful that they did.

However, the fact that the condo was in Mentor—which is about 30 miles east of where I had been living and where all my friends lived—didn't go over very big with everyone.

They thought I was crazy doing all this "for a dog," and there were times when I wondered what I was doing myself. But then I would look at Max and know that I was doing the right thing—for both of us.

Next came the move. Did I mention that I absolutely hate moving? It's a huge amount of work and I was more than tired of it after the last move three years ago.

Fortunately, that last back-breaking move—from a big house full of stuff that we had somehow managed to collect over the last twenty years—had required that I get rid of a lot of things I no longer needed. So this move—I hoped—would be easier since I had a lot less stuff.

But, once again, I was downsizing so I would have a lot less space and more purging of the unnecessary would be required.

This was back in the summer of 2004, and at that point I hadn't begun to realize the great benefits of getting rid of stuff you no longer need. I have since—although I still find it challenging at times.

I love the results, but the process can be tough. I think it's because I learned at an early age to attach emotions to my possessions, and then it's hard to give them up because it's actually emotionally painful—it feels like a loss.

But I'm happy to say that I am getting better at it all

the time. Now I realize that I was just hording things unnecessarily and keeping someone else from using them. So I decided that was pretty silly and now I can release them much more easily. And the move to Mentor for Max was just one more important step in that process.

Remember our closet analogy—you have to get rid of stuff before you can reorganize it and make it more functional.

And that includes extra emotional stuff as well.

Twenty

So Max and I moved to Mentor. With, I might add, some help from my friend Bob, who lives in Florida most of the year. He made a special trip up just to help us move, and it really was a very big help.

A lot of people were surprised that I chose to move to Mentor because they felt it is so "out in the sticks," and I had lived and worked closer to Cleveland for almost thirty years.

I wasn't sure what to expect myself, but Mentor seemed perfectly nice to me—and it was the only choice I had at the time.

Another little irony in the whole situation: I had been living at the Village Green Apartments and the only place I could find to move to was the Village Greene Condos.

I have since concluded that the universe was tired of being subtle with me and just made it real obvious where I was suppose to go. And given the state I was in at that time, they were right.

So Max and I settled in and began our new life together.

Twenty-One

Since the condo didn't have a fenced-in yard, I had no

choice but to walk him several times a day. You could say that this was another smart move on the universe's part since it helped us to bond, and it required that I train him. It also gave us some good exercise, which we both needed.

From the first time I had walked him, however, I had noticed that his back was not straight and that he tended to drag one of his back legs. This really concerned me and I wasn't sure if anything could be done about it.

Fortunately, we found Dr. Neal Sivula, a wonderful veterinarian who specializes in canine chiropractic care, and he was able to straighten Max's back after several treatments. Now I take Max into see him about every six to eight months for him to give Max a tune-up on his spine and everything seems to be working fine.

Another little sign that I was following the right path was the fact that Dr. Sivula's practice was called Dancing Dogs Animal Wellness Center, and I love to dance. That just made me smile. He also recommended Dr. Debbie Ting at Lakeshore Animal Hospital as our regular vet, and she was able to help me with his weight and other issues.

With his back problem fixed, it soon became clear that Max enjoyed the walks—and the training exercises we did on our walks—very much. He was eager to please, and therefore, fairly easy to train. I checked out some books from the library and began training him in earnest that summer.

Because I was interested in getting him certified by Therapy Dogs International (TDI) to do pet therapy work, I also looked into the American Kennel Club (AKC) training program and we began training for their Canine Good Citizen test. I didn't have his AKC papers, but I was able to register him with the AKC as a provisional dog so they could certify him after he passed the test.

After working with him over the summer, I enrolled us in a training class at our local pet store so he could become socialized with other dogs. He had really only been around Rhymer and Seager, and our neighbor Marilyn's dog, Gus, a small Westie, so I thought it would be a good idea for him to learn to be around other dogs as well.

And he loved it. He loved every minute of the two-hour class, although I was exhausted by the time it was over.

Max had no idea, apparently, of how big a dog he was in contrast to the other dogs in the class. And when he got excited, he liked to jump up and down like his four legs had become pogo sticks.

While endearing to me, it tended to scare the owners of the smaller dogs in the class, and for good reason. Max could easily injure a smaller dog with this jumping up and down behavior, even if it was an accident. He certainly didn't have a mean bone in his body, so he would never intentionally hurt another dog, but that didn't mean that he couldn't hurt them by accident.

So my job, obviously, was to keep him under control and at a safe distance from the smaller dogs. Which was easier said than done with a dog that was now pretty strong after several months of intensive daily exercise.

I think Max's size will always be an issue. He is a very handsome, well-built specimen of the canine species, but he is big enough to make most people pause and look in wonder.

I remember one day when I had Max with me in the office of the campground where we were staying and another camper walked in and asked me where his saddle was—and this was from a big guy. Men tended to respond to Max with a little more comfort than women, so this was really surprising. But I don't think he meant as an insult, just as a comment on his size.

I mention Max's size because it was an issue early on in shaping the direction of my life—such as the need to move to Mentor, the need to use the motorhome to travel, and the need to exercise and train him so intensively—and it remains a guiding factor in my life today.

I would probably never have chosen such a big dog on my own, so I can only conclude that the universe knows best and is using "big Max" to guide me on my path.

And over the four years that we have been together, I can state for a fact that Max has taught me how to face and overcome a lot of big fears and I've come to believe that it was not an accident that he arrived in the size of package that he did.

It's like that expression "God (or the universe) works in mysterious ways." I have come to appreciate the truth in that statement and to stop wondering why God or the universe brings what it does into my life. I just try to surrender to it, and to accept whatever comes with grace and gratitude.

One of the things that I've come to accept is Max's puppy personality inside of a big dog. And I'm happy to report we did fine in the pet training once I was able to relax a little and trust that I could manage him in that situation.

Dogs can sense our emotions, so I'm sure that as I became more confident and relaxed, he felt more secure as well.

I have learned that facing tough or scary situations stretches me. It does build my confidence and inner sense of self. And Max, as the well-mannered dog that he has become, constantly reminds me of that growth.

Twenty-Two

Back to our motorhome adventure—where were we? Oh yes, at Myrtle Beach.

We stayed a week at the campground at Myrtle Beach, and I spent a fair amount of that time learning about the motorhome.

I really wanted—and had made a commitment to myself—to learn how to operate the outside part of the motorhome as well as I did the inside. And it was warm enough now that I could dewinterize it without worrying about a freeze.

But I didn't know how.

I had asked in the office about local RV service places, and they had recommended a service that would come out and make repairs at the campground. So I called them and they were happy to come by and help me out.

I had taken the motorhome to Mentor RV Service Center earlier in the fall, and had them winterize it for me since I wasn't sure what to do. They had used the traditional method of pouring RV antifreeze into the fresh water tank and then using the internal water pump to pump the antifreeze into the lines.

So now I needed to get it out of the lines and the fresh water hoses hooked up.

Motorhomes have two sources of water: 1) a fresh water tank that travels with you so you have water all the time by using the electric water pump; and 2) you can hook up to an outside water line at a campsite and then it is just like a house—water comes out of the facets without needing to use the water pump.

You have both hot and cold running water because the

motorhome also has a hot water heater that holds six gallons, but it is constantly being refilled with water and reheats in a short amount of time.

If you're traveling in freezing weather, it's not advisable to use the fresh water pump because the water in the tank could be frozen. In that case, you revert to bottled water for drinking and jugs of water for other purposes. You also don't have any hot water since the hot water heater is emptied as part of the winterizing process.

Since I had traveled the entire trip using only bottled water and a couple of jugs of fresh water, I was more than ready to have the luxury of running water and hot water to boot. It is really a great feeling to take a nice warm shower in your own home on wheels before you go to bed, rather than hiking over to the campground showers.

So I was really ready to get the motorhome fully set up.

The RV repair van pulled up and Max gave them a thorough inspection—which they passed with flying colors since they had learned to carry dog treats in their pockets. The two men said they both had dogs and were not afraid of my big guy.

There are several ways to dewinterize a motorhome, but probably the best is to flush the antifreeze out of the water lines and down through the sewer lines. You do this by hooking up the sewer hoses and opening the valves to drain both the gray and black water tanks. Then you add fresh water to the fresh water tank and use the water pump to move the water through the lines until all of the antifreeze is gone.

Another way is to "blow out the lines" with a compressor. This is the method that the RV repair guys decided to use that day since it is normally quicker. The downside is that it puts a lot of pressure on all of the lines, and they forgot to open my outside water faucets—the motorhome has a little outside shower hose for quick cleaning. And, you guessed it; it blew one of the faucets right off.

I didn't know enough at that point to realize that it was their error—or at least they contributed to the problem. So they replaced the faucet unit and charged me for it.

But I knew that something wasn't quite right with all that and it just redoubled my commitment to learn how these systems worked and to be able to do it myself.

And that is exactly what I have done. Now I know how to winterize and dewinterize the motorhome myself and it is no big deal.

Twenty-Three

With the dewinterizing complete, we were now a fairly functional campsite. This was the first time I had ever tried to do all this on my own, and I was beginning to get the hang of it.

Things that we aren't familiar with can be more intimidating than they need to be. Once I actually got into it, it wasn't that difficult. The idea of it was a lot scarier than the reality.

Not that I was exactly "Ms. Motorhome" by that point. I had managed to figure out how to get the electric, water and sewer systems set up, but using the propane system was still out of my comfort zone.

Propane is normally a very safe gas, and I have lived with natural gas appliances much of my life. But I didn't have to light them on a regular basis to make them work.

I had lit a hot water heater a few times before when I had stayed in a trailer parked by a lake, but, once again, it was my friend, Bob, who really did all that and I mostly watched. But I didn't watch all that often. And, I must confess, when I stayed out at the trailer by myself, I didn't attempt to use the propane. I had a little one-burner electric plate that served my needs just fine.

So for that week at Myrtle Beach, I went back to that system and only used electrical power. And it was just fine. I was only making tea in the morning and simple meals at night so the little electric plate was more than adequate.

Today, I'm happy to report, I feel very comfortable using the propane system, including lighting the hot water heater. But it took me several years to get there.

Again, I think the lesson that I learned was to keep facing my fears—bit by bit—until they are dissolved.

I was committed to learning how to use all of the systems of the motorhome, and that is what I've accomplished because I stuck with it and didn't let my fears defeat me.

I was also learning to ask for help when I needed it.

I tend to try and do everything on my own, and that just wasn't possible in this situation. There was so much I didn't know about the motorhome that I didn't have a choice but to ask for help and learn as I went along.

As I sat at my little dinette table that evening while watching the sun set over the dunes, I again felt this almost over-whelming sense of peace. It had been quite a challenge getting there, but I couldn't have been happier.

It was as if I was climbing some mountain and I had just reached another important summit. I felt such a feeling of contentment and satisfaction.

Yes, I said to myself, you've done it. You're finally where you've wanted to be for so long—in the motorhome by the sea. Now you can really get to work tomorrow on those journals.

Twenty-Four

The next day was Sunday, March 20th, which was the Vernal (Spring) Equinox that year.

The equinox occurs twice each year—once in the spring and once in the fall. It is the time of the year when the length of the day equals the length of the night.

I have come to see those two days as representative of harmony and balance between daylight and darkness in nature, and have celebrated them for many years as symbolic of the way I would like to live my life: focused, centered and balanced.

I also created The Equinox Group as the name of my company when I set it up in 1994. And the mission of my company has been to conduct projects that enhance harmony on the planet.

So it seemed especially symbolic and fitting that I was starting the review of my journals on that special day.

I wanted to review the journals that I had been writing for several years in order to capture the insights and ideas that I had been given while I was journaling.

I have come to believe that we are all much more intuitive than we realize, and that we can hear our inner wisdom if we are open to it and take the time to be still enough to receive it.

That is what journaling does for me—it creates an opening into my inner wisdom. And I thought that some of the insights that I had been given over the years were pretty good. But I tended to forget them soon after I wrote them down, so I thought it would be worthwhile to go through the journals and recapture what I had learned.

I put a tablecloth on the picnic table in our yard and

brought out the boxes of journals that I'd brought along in the motorhome. As I began to read through them, however, I began to feel very anxious and had to stop.

Pretty soon I decided that I really needed to take Max for a walk on the beach.

As we walked, I calmed down and realized that my anxiety was from going back over all the emotional stuff that I had recorded in my journals. It was bringing back all the memories and the feelings that went along with them.

The process that I have been experiencing for the last decade or so has involved going through and sorting out a lot of old emotional wounds, as I described earlier with the "cleaning out the closet" analogy.

And I had recorded a lot of it in my journals along with all the great insights, so I was wading through all that muck again in order to find the nuggets of truth that I knew were valuable. And I guess I wasn't prepared to relive all that—at least not at that moment.

Walking with Max on the beach helped a lot. Being by the sea is very therapeutic for me—it reminds me of just how small we humans are in the grand scheme of things when I look out over the vast ocean and endless horizon.

That perspective is very helpful because it reminds me not to take myself too seriously. How can my little problems and fears be of that great of importance in comparison to the vastness and timelessness of the universe?

So I prayed for support and guidance, and returned to the motorhome to try it again.

And this time it was better. I could only read a few pages at a time, but that was OK since it was all I planned on doing while I was there, and I had decided to stay for the rest of the week.

I had debated about going further south to get into even warmer weather, but everything seemed to be telling me to stay put.

When I had checked in, I had told them I would be staying two or three days—just long enough to get the systems put together and do a little reorganizing inside the motorhome. And then I would hit the road again and go on to Georgia or even into Florida to get some really hot days. Even though it was getting to be near the end March, the weather had only been in the high 60's in the Carolinas.

And I didn't think staying longer at that campground was really an option given how crowded they were. But when I checked with the office, I was told that I could stay for the rest of the week and that they would give me a free day—pay for six days and the seventh was free.

And that seventh day happened to be my birthday so it only seemed fitting to accept their generosity—and the universe's guidance—and stay there for the rest of the week.

So I had several days to review my journals, and decided just to take it a little bit at a time.

By the end of the day, I had put together a nice little patio outside the motorhome, including an outdoor carpet, a couple of chairs and the tablecloth on the picnic table— very homey.

And I had also gone through about half of the first of two boxes of journals, and had recorded a lot of useful ideas. And, I'm happy to report, without experiencing another anxiety attack.

Twenty-Five

Since it was a Sunday, I had also attended the church service that morning at the little open-air chapel on the campground—with Max since dogs were welcome—and the minister had talked about "letting God lead our lives."

That was exactly what I had been trying to learn to do, but I was finding it easier said than done.

I have been so conditioned to believe that I should have control over my life, and that we need to maintain that control no matter what.

I think that is why I tended to find change so unsettling. It made me feel like things were out of control in my life, and it scared me.

So turning control of my life over to God or the divine universe or anyone else was very frightening to me.

I had learned to do it somewhat when I was on those earlier driving quests and things always worked out great. But then I would come home and fall right back into the old "I'm in charge" mindset.

But here I was on quest number four and the minister is telling me once again that this is the way to inner peace and contentment. It was like God was sitting on my shoulder and whispering it directly into my ear.

I realized right then and there that I knew this intellectually to be true, but I hadn't fully accepted it in my heart. It was in my head but not my heart, and I knew I would never be able to fully live that way until my head and my heart were united in this belief.

In reviewing my journals that week at the beach, I realized that I had been working on this integration for a long time. But I also realized that I wasn't there yet.

One of the other things that I learned from that review is that the "cleansing of the old emotional wounds" was creating a more loving me—like it was cleaning out room in my heart to be more loving towards myself and everyone else in my world.

And Max, of course, was facilitating this process big time—he was not only constantly giving me lots of unconditional love, but he was also teaching me how to give a lot of unconditional love back to him.

Big dog, big love.

Once again I was reminded of the purpose of having Max in my life, and how important a role he was playing in helping me become a more loving and conscious human being.

I think that was the day I really began to think of him as an angel guiding me on my path, and I believe it even more so today.

The Spring Equinox in 2005 was a very big day for me.

It was the beginning of the realization of how far I had come and yet also where I needed to go. It also planted the seed to write about my experiences so that other people might learn something that would help them on their own journey.

As I said that day in my journal, *the real gift that I think you want me to deliver is helping people to move from their head to their heart—and give them courage that they can, using my own experience as an example. It's not really about me; it's about helping people know that it can be done and that they can do it.*

And that is how this book came to be.

Twenty-Six

After such a full day and all that sea air, Max and I went to bed early that night. But about 1 am, I was back up making myself a cup of herbal tea. I couldn't sleep because I had begun to cough badly from a cold that I had picked up a few days earlier.

But I wasn't too surprised by the cold either.

By this point, I was beginning to appreciate that everything that came into my life came for a reason, and I had a pretty good idea of what lesson this cold was bringing with it: take better care of your body.

I wondered if my "dis-ease" wasn't a message to become more conscious of my body and to stop ignoring what I was doing to it by regularly eating and drinking more than I needed. And, yes, I had packed on the pounds and was pretty unhappy about that too.

About seven years earlier, I had begun to feel heavy even though I was pretty slim. It was a very strange sensation that I will never forget.

I remember dressing for an important occasion and feeling certain that I wouldn't be able to wear one of my favorite dresses because I was too fat. But I could wear it with no problem—which only made me feel even stranger.

It was like I knew I was going to get heavy no matter what I did.

I have had a hypothyroid condition since I was a teenager, and had been on medication for it for years. So I thought maybe my dosage was off and that was the problem. I had gone to see my doctor, but he had found nothing wrong with my thyroid or anything else. And he couldn't understand my concerns since I looked slim and healthy to him.

And it didn't figure that it was what I was eating and drinking since I was doing both in moderation at that point in time, and exercising regularly as well.

But I still had that sensation of heaviness, and it wasn't going away.

And, sure enough, over the next eight years I gained about thirty pounds—which is quite a lot for a woman who is only five foot three inches tall.

Now, I'm not suggesting that this is a necessary part of everyone's process—I'm pretty sure it isn't—but it was a part of mine.

But it also came about as a result of my eating and drinking habits—which went from pretty healthy to pretty neglectful over this period of time. I used food and wine to comfort myself as I was going through this period of darkness, and the need for comfort far outweighed the need to take care of myself.

I mention this not because I'm proud of it—I'm not—but because it may save someone else from going down that same road. Or if you do go down it, go down it consciously and be as kind as you can to yourself.

I firmly believe that a big part of my being stuck in that place of darkness for so long was the terrible mental thrashings that I would give myself out of guilt over my choices.

I have since come to see that being so judgmental and harsh towards myself was not helpful at all; in fact, I'm sure it was very detrimental.

A very big part of this process, for me, has been learning to love myself and accept everything about myself—and I mean everything. We are imperfect human beings and we always will be, but that does not mean that we cannot come to accept and love ourselves completely.

I now understand that you can become a conscious, loving being without needing to become perfect.

The idea that one has to become perfect before they are good enough to become conscious is an illusion, and one that will keep you trapped forever trying—and never succeeding—to obtain perfection.

The only thing one really needs is to learn to love yourself completely and to accept everyone and everything that comes into your life. You don't have to like everything that happens in your life, you just have to accept it.

That has been a hard lesson for me to learn, and I'm sure that our society's preoccupation with perfection played a role in it as well.

But whatever the reasons, I wrote a lot of journal pages where I identified and berated every imperfection of myself that I could think of. But I have finally learned to let it all go and accept myself just as I am.

And what a relief that has been—I no longer beat myself up over anything.

It took me several years of "practice" to get to this point since the pattern was so entrenched, but I eventually taught myself to stop doing it.

The practice was to catch myself when I was doing it and just try and stop, or even find the positive in the situation. My mind would try to keep doing it, so I had to learn to be very patient with myself when it slipped back into that pattern.

Eventually, I was able to watch and really manage my thoughts, and now I only occasionally laugh at my mind when it attempts to be critical. And if I can learn to retrain the way my mind works, so can you, and you may be doing it already.

And it is a lot nicer place to live.

Twenty-Seven

The cold that I had the week I was at Myrtle Beach helped me learn that lesson even more clearly.

It is so easy to be critical of yourself when you're sick—after all, you're not being productive, and we often attach a lot of quilt to that.

I know for myself that, in the past, sometimes being sick was the only time I allowed myself to really relax and stop worrying about everything and everybody else.

And that is a sad way to live.

As I sat drinking my tea that night I realized that this was exactly the way I had been living for way too long. "I must be busy and productive at all times or I am worthless," was my unconscious mindset.

I realized that my busy-busy routine was really blocking me from becoming more conscious. How could I be conscious with all that mental noise constantly going around in my head?

Sitting there in the silence I felt at peace.

And that is when I realized that I would never become the conscious, loving person I wanted to be if I didn't slow down, and "quiet down."

I also realized that the choice to slow down and quiet down was not the way the mainstream worked, and clearly went against the grain of the model of success that most of us have been raised to believe in.

Multi-tasking is the way to go, and the busier you are the more important you are. It seems like we are all getting so busy with all our electronic devices that we are driving silence right out of our lives.

And with it, our sense of peace and contentment.

I took my cup of tea outside to sit with Max on our new little patio and gaze up at the sky. The stars looked huge and like I could reach up and touch them. The campground was dark and quiet—and I could hear the gentle and rhythmic lap of the waves on the beach.

Now this is peace, I thought to myself.

I was completely awe struck by the beauty and vastness of the night sky. "Thank you, God, for getting me up and outside to see this—it's well worth a little cough," I thought to myself quietly.

That night taught me a lesson that I will never forget. *Slow down, be quiet and look up into the sky more often.* Those three things have taught me how to ground myself, and keep my life in proper perspective.

Twenty-Eight

The next few days passed very quickly.

We had developed a nice routine: early morning walk on the beach, breakfast, work time for me/nap for Max, another walk on the beach, lunch, more work/nap time, and then dinner and another walk on the beach or around the campground.

Max absolutely loved the beach. I put him on a long 20-foot leash and wore my water shoes so we could both go splashing in the waves.

I would like to have taken him off the leash but there were a lot of people around, and I had learned that not everyone wants a 100-pound dog barreling up to them to say hello. And quite a few of the people out walking were older, and I didn't want to take the chance that Max might accidentally knock them down.

But we had a grand time on our walks, and he always enjoyed playing with the other dogs that we met along the way.

I had taught Max to stand by my side and let the other dog approach us since the other dogs were usually a lot smaller than Max. And once they had "smelled their hellos," I would release him and let him run around with them.

This actually worked pretty well and I was getting fairly cocky about my well-trained dog until one day when we were out walking and spotted a woman walking her Golden Retriever towards us.

The dog looked friendly so we went into our "meet and greet" routine. I had hooked my left hand under Max's collar to keep him still and up close by my side. And everything seemed to be going fine until the woman reached down and unleashed her dog when they were about 20 feet away from us.

The dog charged towards Max ready for a good romp and to smell his hello, and Max responded by twisting around to meet the other dog head on—only my hand was still in his collar. In the blink of an eye, my hand was caught in a vise being pulled tighter and tighter as Max struggled to get loose and go after the other dog.

"Ouch," does not begin to describe the pain I was in. It took me several seconds that felt more like hours to get my hand free and I knew I was hurt. I put my hand down into a pool of cool sea water and that made it feel a little better.

But not much.

The woman apologized for her dog's behavior and they walked on down the beach. I gathered Max's leash back together and headed back to the motorhome, muttering to myself about how some people don't know how to manage their own dogs.

When we got back, I put a bag of Max's frozen green beans on my injured left hand. I give him green beans with his food at dinner to help fill him up and keep his weight down.

The injured area on my hand was mostly my two knuckles—particularly my ring finger—which had been caught in the vise when his collar had twisted so abruptly.

After a while, I realized that the beans were not going to do it, so I went to the campground store and bought a bag of ice. I soaked my hand in a bowl of ice water off and on for several hours, and eventually it started to feel better, although it was still quite swollen.

So now what? Are one or more of my fingers broken? Do I need to see a doctor?

I called the office to ask if they knew of an urgent care center around and, surprisingly, they did not. I had assumed other campers had gotten sick or injured and would have needed such care, but apparently they either called an ambulance or went to the emergency room on their own.

Since I didn't have a car, I would need to drive the motorhome if I could even find some place to go. But by this time it was getting late in the afternoon, and I decided to create a make-shift splint out of chopsticks on my two injured fingers and see how they were in the morning.

I was also tired, in pain, and just not in the mood to try and unhook all the lines with one hand, and then drive the motorhome in rush hour traffic—and I didn't even know where to go.

So we had dinner and went back outside to try and relax and enjoy the evening on our little outdoor patio.

But my mood was anything but peaceful.

I remembered the awesome feeling of peace that I had felt sitting under the stars the night before, but I was miles away from it.

I was angry with the woman who let her dog off the leash—the accident wasn't Max's or the other dog's fault—they had just done what dogs do. Maybe if she had warned me that she was going to take her dog off its leash, I would have been prepared and could have taken my hand out from under his collar in time.

So I sat there stewing in my resentment.

And then I laughed because I remembered that resentment was the very topic of my journaling that morning.

Twenty-Nine

At 7 am that morning, the sun had filled the motorhome with this beautiful white light that was shining directly on us as I sat with Max on the sofa.

"Search your heart for resentments. Heal your heart—search out the resentments and let them go—that is the way your heart will heal—and consciousness is through the healed heart," was the message given to me as we sat in that beautiful light.

So I had listed all of my resentments in full detail. But in looking them back over, I realized that all of these resentments were about my disappointment that these people hadn't done or acted the way that I had wanted them to behave.

Then I realized that these resentments were all really pretty silly—these people were all just doing their own thing like I was doing mine.

I had ended that journaling session with a prayer: "*Dear God, please help me release these lingering resentments so that I might serve you with a full and healed heart. Amen.*"

And here I was, twelve hours later, filled again with a powerful resentment towards the woman who had caused the injury to my hand.

"Well," I said to myself, "I guess you gave me another lesson in letting go of resentments now didn't you God. OK, I forgive that woman but I still think she acted like an idiot."

"That won't do now will it," my inner wisdom whispered.

"No, I don't suppose it will. OK, I forgive her and thank her for bringing me this important lesson. Will that do?"

"As long as you really mean it."

Actually, I didn't really mean it at the time. I tried but it's not that easy—at least for me—to learn these lessons right after I hear them. It seems like it has taken me several years and many such experiences to really get to the point where I can fully accept them in my heart.

It takes time to fully heal your heart. But I learned that day that it is a necessary part of the consciousness process, and a goal well worth pursuing.

Thirty

The week at Myrtle Beach was not all sweetness and light. I found myself in the darkness as well.

The task of reviewing my journals had unlocked some powerful, negative emotions and I was beginning to wonder where the heck I was going with all of this "consciousness process" anyway.

About the fourth night there, I was feeling very out of sorts, and I wanted to smother the feeling with comfort food and wine. Because of my cold, I hadn't had any wine since I got there and I was ready to have some now.

I had realized in reading through those early journals that I had been using a "TV/comfort food/wine routine" to cope with the emotions that I was unearthing.

But I could also see how wine had "opened up the closet door" to let the emotions out in the first place. A lot of those emotions had been buried pretty deeply, and I don't know if I could have accessed them by myself without this help.

Maybe with therapy, but I was doing this "excavating" on almost a daily basis, and it wouldn't have been possible or affordable using traditional therapy.

I believe that emotions have energy or maybe I should say are energy, and as they were being released, energy was being released along with them.

And I realized that I was using wine to both help me release these emotions/energy as well as to smother them—or contain them at a level that I could handle.

It was like I could only physically handle so much energy being released at one time and still stay in any way functional in the world.

I have heard of people who have had a "sudden and rapid conversion into consciousness" and I would guess that they had a huge release of emotional energy all at once. But it also apparently made it difficult for them to function in the real world—although that world no longer mattered much to them anyway.

But it still mattered to me, and I was still trying to keep some level of control over myself. Like a tea kettle letting off steam a little bit at a time. I didn't want the whole thing to blow up and burn me in the process.

From the review of the journals I had done over the last several days, it was clear that my process was more like the children's game of "chutes and ladders"—climbing up on the ladder of awareness/consciousness only to hit a rough spot and go sliding back down the chute.

It felt like a crazy upward then downward motion, although it was always slightly higher with each effort. Like a zig-zag pattern up the side of a mountain.

And I was using wine to both help me climb as well as to not climb too high or too fast.

So here I was at Myrtle Beach, trying to climb a really big mountain and I had no wine.

"Why can't I crack through this?" I asked myself in my journal that night. "Why am I even here? Every time I read my journals I get depressed at how long I've been dealing with the same stuff. Is this review really helpful or am I just going to feel angry with myself about it?"

My angels, my divine inner wisdom—or whomever that voice belonged to—responded by saying "it took Peace Pilgrim fifteen years from commitment to practice—why do you think it would be any easier for you? You've made more progress than you realize—try and relax and let it sink in."

But I wasn't buying any of that. "So I read all this and feel angry and lonesome, and wonder what the heck I'm doing here—or with my life in general. Have I just been fooling myself all this time? Does my 'happiness' really revolve around eating fattening things with wine and watching TV—all just to space out?"

"I'm about as spiritual as a sand crab—no, they are at least leading a life with a purpose—unlike me. I'm tired of wallowing around in the past—it only keeps me stuck in pain and anger."

"Which you enjoy," commented my inner voice.

"Because it's what I know. I feel like such a phony, and it's depressing."

"You've come much further than you realize. Maybe it's the remark by Peace Pilgrim (I had watched a video of her life earlier in the day) of being considered odd that has upset you. And yes, that will happen and if acceptance by the 'tribe' is that important to you, then you will remain stuck between these two worlds—and continue your pattern of hiding behind your TV/comfort food/wine routine. What's it going to be?"

"Is that what this is? More 'please accept me' behavior? I think I can deal with that—I guess I can accept being considered odd," I wrote.

This mini-meltdown was just one of many that I've experienced as I've walked this path. But each one has forced me to confront some barrier that was holding me back—and as that barrier was confronted, it dissolved, and I could walk forward with a clearer and lighter heart.

I share this darker part of the process with you out of my commitment to the truth of my experience. It would have been easier to just write about the good times but that wouldn't have given you the full picture. And, in the end, I realized just how healing these dark periods were, and how they opened my heart in a big way to let in even more love and light.

Thirty-One

By the end of the week at Myrtle Beach, I had reviewed all of my journals and had put together a nice list of the insights and ideas that I wanted to remember.

It was a very meaningful time in my life—I had faced my fear of driving and using the motorhome, I had faced my fear of my past, and I had come to appreciate just how far I had actually traveled on my spiritual path.

I knew I wasn't done yet—maybe one is never really done—but it was a time to celebrate what I had achieved.

That was my birthday present to myself—a big pat on the back for having the courage to commit to this path and the courage to face the many fears that served both as barriers and as booster rockets along the way.

My other birthday present was Max—I had enjoyed him so much that week at the beach and I was sure he had a good time too. Just being with him was opening my heart and healing it at the same time.

I also thanked God, the angels and everyone else up there that was helping me along the way.

One thing had become very clear to me and that is that we are never alone on our journey. We have a lot of help, support and guidance available to us if we can only open ourselves to receive it.

And, ironically, I was going to learn that very lesson even more clearly in the days ahead.

Thirty-Two

We left Myrtle Beach and headed south on Highway 19. The weather had been sunny but still cool while we were there, and I was eager to get into warmer weather.

But the day proved to be rainy and stormy so we pulled up after only a few hours of driving to stay overnight in a Wal-Mart parking lot in Georgetown, South Carolina. It wasn't my first choice, but the storm had grown in intensity and I decided I just needed to get off the road and bed down for the night.

I was slowly learning to respect the weather and the road conditions, and decided it would be better to be safe than sorry.

Before we left the campground, I had filled the fresh water tank up about half full so we would have water that night. I turned on the generator in order to heat a little supper up in the microwave and warm up the bed. It was a cold rain and the motorhome had gotten a little chilly as well.

The next day dawned sunny and a little warmer so we ate a quick breakfast and got back on the road.

But not before I almost backed us up into a ditch.

I am strongly committed to recycling and I had gathered quite a bit of it while we were at Myrtle Beach. I had been keeping it in plastic bags and had stored them in the shower. But that was not convenient when I wanted to take a shower so I thought now would be a good time to drop them off at a recycling center.

I had seen a sign that pointed out the direction to a recycling center the night before. So I decided to look for it again before we got back on the highway.

Unfortunately, I missed the sign because we were going in the opposite direction, so I decided to go down a side street to turn around and try finding it again. But the street I turned down was apparently a dead end—a long street but no side streets.

So I had no choice but to try and turn the motorhome around using someone's driveway. This wouldn't have been a problem except that there was a four-foot deep ditch on either side of the street—which I had not really noticed.

I found a relatively large driveway and pulled in as far as I could go—which was about two-thirds of the motorhome. Then I put it in reverse and backed it up—trying very hard not to take out the neighbor's mailbox.

So I thought I was doing OK, but something made me stop and go outside and take a look—and I about fainted. I was within a few inches of having my two huge rear tires in the ditch.

I really don't know what made me stop and look, but I started thanking the heavens right then and there. I can't imagine how they would have been able to pull me out of that ditch if I had gone into it. A very big tow truck and a lot of money probably.

So I tried to breathe again—the sight of the motorhome on the edge of that ditch had sucked the air right out of me—and I slowly moved the motorhome forward and backward until I got it turned around. There was a ditch in front of me as well, so my available turning area was very limited.

I did make the turn into the recycling center on the next try, and was able to contribute my bags of plastic bottles to them. Recycling has been a commitment of mine for many years, and I continue it today—no matter how challenging it is to find recycling centers along the way.

Needless to say, I was very grateful to my "travel angels" for leading me out of that tight spot, and I promised them that I would get a statue of an angel when I got home, and put it in the motorhome out of appreciation.

And I did. I found a lovely brass sculpture of an angel and I hung it on one of the walls in the motorhome—and it continues to guide and protect us every day on all of our travels.

Thirty-three

We continued on our way—with me shaken up a bit—and ended up in a nice campground a little south of Charleston, South Carolina. I had been in that area during an earlier driving quest and had found that area, known as the low country, very appealing.

It was still early afternoon when we pulled in, since I was beginning to realize the virtue of stopping earlier in the day. It made driving less tiring, and gave Max and me a chance to actually enjoy walking around the campground. We didn't have any real schedule to keep so what was the point of driving until we dropped?

And after the ditch experience, I was ready to call it a day pretty early.

As we drove in and parked in our assigned spot, I noticed a few people nearby staring in our direction. It turns out that they thought that a young girl was driving the motorhome since I had my hair in a ponytail and was wearing sunglasses and I'm not very big.

They all came over when we came out and had a good laugh about it. But it was also another one of those "where's your husband honey? And do you need help getting set up?"

I told them no thank you, but I was still pretty green at doing all the connections, so it took me quite a while. But I got it done and took Max on a nice long walk around the campground. They even had a fenced play area for dogs so he got in some good ball chasing time.

By suppertime, however, I was beginning to wonder again what I was doing. The old "what's the plan" attitude was rearing its ugly head and I had no answer for it. I had intentionally decided to travel without a plan for a few days in the motorhome before heading back north to Mentor, but I was beginning to feel a little bit lost.

So I took out the big road atlas and considered our options. I also turned on the TV to the Weather Channel—one of my favorites—to see how the weather was up north. It was nearing the end of March, but I didn't want to bring the motorhome back if the roads were going to be bad.

We really hadn't had any really warm weather on the whole trip—which was disappointing to me. So I was very tempted to continue to go south and get some warm sunshine on myself before I went back home.

Max and I looked at the atlas, and I explained our various choices to him. "We can go south and get into the sunshine or we can begin to wind our way home—what do you vote?" He answered with a big yawn.

After a few more minutes of thinking about my options, I realized that I was tired too. It had been a challenging trip in many ways and I began to realize that I was running out of energy.

The thought of continuing to go south was appealing, but it also felt very demanding. It is a lot more work to travel every day in a motorhome than it is to park and stay in one place for a week. Every day you have to unhook everything and hook it all up again at night.

I could see that I had gotten spoiled by our week at Myrtle Beach—one set-up and we were good to go. This making camp twice every day was something else again.

And my injured hand was better but not great yet, so all that hooking and unhooking of the lines was not appealing.

In fact, I was beginning to realize that I really needed a doctor to look at my hand and probably get it x-rayed just to be on the safe side—which I did after we got home to Mentor. It turned out that nothing was broken, but it was sore for quite a while. But every time it hurt, it reminded me of the lesson on resentment, and I could practice forgiveness a little bit more.

After thinking all this through, I decided to slowly make our way north so we could spend a few days in a campground if we liked it and still be home by early April.

Thirty-Four

And we found just such a campground the next day in Pinehurst, North Carolina. Being a golf fan, I had seen on TV the lovely golf courses at Pinehurst, and the PGA was scheduled to play the U.S. Open there in July. So I thought it would be fun to go check it out for myself.

It turned out that the roads in the Village of Pinehurst looked a little too tight for me to drive the motorhome through so I never really saw the golf courses there. But our handy Woodall's had several RV campgrounds listed in that area.

The one we found was picture perfect—beautiful pine trees and a lovely little lake. It wasn't that full because it was actually off-season until the first of April, so we were able to get a nice campsite with a lovely view of the lake.

We liked it so much that we ended up staying there for three days. The sun had come out and was nice and warm so we finally felt like were "on holiday." There was something about a hot sun that I found very appealing at that point—I just needed to warm my bones for some reason.

After that successful respite, I felt eager to hit the road again—but first we were going to be saved by the travel angels once again.

Pinehurst is located off the beaten path so I had driven the back roads to get there. Which is actually a nice way to travel—it's slower and more scenic. But those winding roads don't lend themselves to driving a motorhome at the speed limit, so I had learned to pull off when I could to let the line of cars behind us pass.

So as we left Pinehurst, we were once again on those country roads and using the gravel shoulder to let cars pass. And somewhere along the way I had picked up a rock in one of my tires—and it must have been a big rock because I could hear it as it hit against the pavement.

"Will it just work its way out of the tire?" I wondered to myself, "or will it puncture it?"

I decided not to take a chance on a punctured tire out in the middle of nowhere so I pulled into a forest ranger station hoping that they might be able to give me a hand.

A nice young man came out and, after I told him about my problem and the fact that I couldn't see the rock to get it out myself, he offered to check it out for us. He asked me to pull the motorhome around and into their big maintenance garage.

He got under the motorhome and found the rock and removed it. So I'm thanking him and offering to pay him for his trouble when he asks me if I've checked the air in the tires lately.

And, of course, I hadn't. Although I did have the tires,

brakes, and all the fluid levels checked by an RV service center before I began the trip. So I figured I'd be OK. Again, thinking of the motorhome more like a car than the vehicle it actually is.

So he offered to check the tires for me and—much to my horror—found that I had almost no air in one of the inner back tires. Motorhomes have two tires in the front and four tires in the rear—double tires on each side to carry the extra weight.

Needless to say, you don't want to be driving a 16,000 pound motorhome with one of the back tires almost flat. I couldn't see that tire because it was on the inside, but there are valves that extend from both tires that you can use to check the tire pressure. But I didn't know—until then—that I should do it on a regular basis.

So he checked and filled all the tires to their recommended level, and we were ready to roll once again. He refused payment saying he was happy to help and that is what they were there for.

I must confess that I felt a bit shaken by that situation, and very, very grateful that the rock had led me to ask for help.

And there was not a doubt in my mind that the travel angels were once again responsible for getting the tire taken care of before it became a big problem—and us safely on the road again.

Thirty-Five

I know that my belief in angels traveling with us is only my opinion, and that many people would just write it off as luck or good fortune that the tire problem had been caught in time.

And that's fine—everyone should believe whatever they are

comfortable believing. I'm not trying to convince anyone of anything. I just know how I felt during those situations and they have made a believer out of me.

I had a strange feeling of lightness as we left the forest station. It was as if I was lit up inside with tremendous gratitude and appreciation to the universe for the good care that it was taking of us on our little adventure.

And that feeling pretty much stayed with me the remainder of our journey back to Mentor.

The whole trip was a real adventure and journey of personal discovery. It was as if my human skepticism had been cracked wide open and I just would never doubt the universe again. I know that it's hard to fully communicate that feeling, but it was powerful enough for me to say that I believe that the trip profoundly altered my life—for the better.

As I pulled the motorhome up in front of our condo in Mentor several days later, I knew without a doubt that the trip had made me into a different person and also brought me closer to Max. All of the challenges and fears that we had faced had paid off: I felt more grounded and content than I had ever felt in my life and more connected to the divine as well.

In every walk with nature one receives far more than he seeks.

Muir

You have to learn how to fall before you can fly.

Paul Simon

Part Two

March, 2008.

My hands were shaking. Uncontrollably it seemed. I could just imagine what my voice was going to sound like if my nerves were going this wild.

Because I was about to stand up and sing karaoke style—for the first time ever.

In case you are unfamiliar with karaoke, it is when you stand up in front of people and sing the lead vocals to the words that are shown on the karaoke machine. The machine provides the words, the timing, and the background music—but you have to sing the lead part of the song.

Why, you might be asking yourself—why does anyone ever do this potentially very embarrassing activity?

They say singing karaoke is a lot of fun—and it had been fun watching people do it for the last two months. That is what finally drove me to take the leap and try to do it myself.

I've always loved to sing and people have told me that I have a decent voice, but my singing career has been limited to humming along with the car radio or singing along with a favorite CD.

We had been going to karaoke night at the Moose and the Elk Lodges for the last several weeks, and I couldn't stand it any longer.

I need to do this, I thought to myself. Or did one of my angels whisper it into my ear? *Face your fear*—I could just hear them saying to me over and over.

So I had decided to do it.

But not without practice. In talking to some of the regulars who have gotten this whole karaoke thing down, they apparently practice quite a bit with their own karaoke machine. And they pick songs that they like and even bring their own CDs along in special cases.

They take this pretty seriously, I thought.

And, oddly, that made me feel a little more comfortable. A project, I thought, I can take this on as a project. I can study it, figure it out, and do it—just like they do.

Sounded good in theory, but I was about to move from theory to reality in two minutes flat. And I wasn't feeling so confident.

The problem was I couldn't back down. Not with half of the room filled with my new Florida friends who were all waiting for me to do something that I had talked about for weeks.

Suddenly I wished that I had gone somewhere else to try and do this for the first time—somewhere that no one had ever seen me before and would never see me again.

"Great time for that idea, I thought to myself. Where were all those good ideas when I needed them, I berated my angels. Aren't you guys supposed to be on top of all this?"

And then the DJ called my name.

"Oh darn" I said to myself—or something along that line.

"You can do this," the voice inside my heart said. "Just get up there and do it—now."

And I did.

And I'd love to say that I was a smash, but I wasn't. I was OK, but only OK.

But I felt great—once my heart stopped racing at 100 miles an hour. I felt like my whole body was smiling from the inside out.

"That wasn't so bad," I thought to myself. "I can do this—just wait until next time."

So my karaoke debut marked another milestone in my life journey—the main theme of which seemed to keep repeating itself: *face your fears and you will grow.*

I was beginning to suspect, however, that there was never going to be an end to the situations the universe could bring me to teach me that lesson. Would I ever graduate from that pattern and just enjoy a peaceful life?

That remains to be seen, but it hasn't happened yet.

But I'm getting ahead of myself. Before I tell you about our RV trip to Florida in 2008, I should share with you our exciting RV adventure in 2006, and our summer as seasonal campers in 2007.

Two

It was February 22, 2006, and we were headed south on our second RV quest. We had once again had to pick a day in between snowstorms to get out of town, and that day looked like the best one for quite a while.

We had gotten a little bit of a late start, leaving Mentor about noon, because the motorhome had been stored several miles away. We were headed south on I-71 and had been traveling for about four hours total, including a stop along the way.

It was a gray day and dusk seemed to be coming early, probably because of the low clouds. Whatever the reason, I didn't want to drive in the dark and a light rain was beginning to fall. It was in the high thirties, but they were predicting freezing rain coming later, so I decided to pull off and park at a truck stop just north of Cincinnati.

I knew I wouldn't be able to use my main power cord, but I had the generator for just such emergencies if the weather really got really cold.

And Max was glad to stop as well. We had stopped at a rest area just north of Columbus about midway in the drive—having learned the lesson of pacing ourselves from our earlier trip—but it was still a long four hours of traveling for both of us.

So I decompressed from travel mode by walking Max around the big grassy area near the truck stop. It had been sunny off and on during the drive, but now the sky was completely gray and I could smell snow in the air.

I was glad that I had decided to stop as the rain started coming down in earnest not long after we climbed back on board.

I fed Max his supper—food always being his first priority and a guaranteed way to keep him happy while I went inside the truck stop. He really was a good traveler and was fairly patient with me as long as I remembered to keep his needs in mind.

So I ran in to use the facilities at the truck stop—yes, the motorhome was still winterized—and to get some warm food for my supper.

I had parked near the restaurant part of the truck stop because I knew that I would need to go in there, but I was wondering if I wanted to park there all night. So I looked the parking lot over, and spotted an ideal place for us to park on the other side of the building.

Not wanting to lose the space, I quickly fired up the

motorhome and moved it over there. We were under a big light for safety, and yet close to where I now knew the restrooms were located in the facility.

"Great," I thought to myself, "this will be just fine" I assured Max.

So I ate my supper and turned on the generator so I could use the little electric heater that I had brought along—as well as warm up the electric heating pad on my bed. It had gotten chilly in the motorhome as darkness fell, and we needed the heat.

We were both tired—or at least I was and Max was always up for curling up with me in my big bed if I let him—so I decided to turn in for the night fairly early.

Everything was nice and snug when I turned off the lights so I shut the generator off thinking the motorhome would hold the heat over night.

Wrong—boy was I wrong.

We woke up with the sun coming through the window— which seemed pleasant—but it was also freezing inside the motorhome.

So cold I could see my breath when I said good morning to Max. Who didn't answer me back except to send me a look that said, "leave me alone I want to sleep some more."

But sleeping any more for me was not in the cards.

Sometime during the night, a big truck had pulled up right along side of us and was running its generator right next to the bedroom window. And those generators are LOUD.

I had intentionally parked away from all the trucks in order to avoid this very problem, and now someone had parked not two feet away from me.

So I was tired from a restless sleep due to the noise and now I was freezing on top of it.

Once again I just had to laugh because I had recently been reading about the importance of "accepting whatever came into your life and the lesson it was intended to bring you."

Right at that moment, however, the theory sounded like hogwash—I was grumpy and cold and was not "accepting and appreciating" it at all.

So I got dressed under the covers—it was that cold—and finally braved dealing with the situation. Max had to go out anyway so I didn't have much choice.

When we got outside, I could see why the truck driver had parked next to me—the whole parking lot was jam packed with trucks—there wasn't a spare inch to be seen anywhere.

It turned out that the weather had gotten a lot colder a lot faster than predicted, and the roads had turned pretty treacherous during the night. Since there aren't a lot of truck stops in that rural area—or anything else for that matter—this truck stop had become very crowded.

As I walked Max on the frosty grass, my mood lightened. The sun was coming up with a beautiful sunrise so I decided to let my irritation go and just figure out how I was going to get warm and get us moving on down the road.

Three

We did eventually get both warm and back on the road— but not for a couple of hours.

There was a thick coating of ice on the windshield that my little internal defroster wasn't making a dent in—not surprising since it was so cold out.

And we were also parked in—there were so many trucks in the lot that they had parked very close to each other and also parked in part of the exit lanes.

My ideal spot of the night before had become much less ideal over night. Now there was barely enough room to squeeze by the big truck next to me—maybe.

While I had gained confidence in my driving over the last year or so, I knew I would be cutting it close if I tried to leave any time soon.

So I decided to stay put, and focus on getting the ice off the windshield. The motorhome is so tall that I would need a ladder—which I didn't have—to reach the windshield to try and scrape it off from the outside.

I turned the generator back on and prayed that the portable heater pointed at the windshield would eventually do the trick.

And it did—about an hour later the ice was melting and I could use the windshield wipers to move it off. And the best news was that the truck next to me had fired up his engine and roared off a short time ago.

Actually, it seemed like there was a continuous exodus of trucks from the lot—truck drivers hit the road early, which worked well for us.

So by about 8 am we were back on I-71 South heading as quickly as we could to warmer weather. We had tentative plans to visit a friend in a week or so at Vero Beach, but our itinerary was intentionally vague—it was another "let's just go exploring" game plan.

But we never would have guessed the unplanned events that would soon occur and which would affect me for the rest of my life.

Four

Our second day of travel went pretty smoothly, and so did the third day until later in the afternoon.

We were barreling down the highway in Georgia when I almost got sideswiped by a driver in a big white SUV who was talking on a cell phone and not watching where they were going.

The speed limit in most of the states in the south is 70 miles an hour, but most of the traffic seemed to be going even faster.

I am most comfortable going about 60 to 65 miles an hour in the motorhome, so it is very stressful trying to drive in those states. And with people whizzing on and off the exits, it gets even more stressful.

By this point, I was hot, I was tired, and now completely frazzled by the near accident. So I tell Max—who is also hot, tired and frazzled by the look of him—that we need to stop.

I love Chick-fil-A sandwiches, and I had seen a billboard advertising the restaurant earlier in the day. "OK Max, the next exit that has a Chick-fil-A sign is for us," I promised him.

And sure enough, the next exit had a sign for the restaurant. Which given everything, had come at just the right time. So we take the exit and then I saw that the town where all the restaurants are located was actually two miles down the road.

"Two miles," I think to myself, "that's a long way to go for a short stop. May be we should just get back on the highway and keep going."

And I almost did. But some little voice inside me said "take a break" and so I made the turn towards the town.

And a few minutes later I am parking the motorhome in the shade in the Target parking lot across from the Chick-fil-A restaurant. I often had to park it in a big lot and walk over to where I wanted to go just to get enough space to get the motorhome in and out easily.

I opened the windows so the motorhome could cool off and be nicer for Max while I went and got us some food. As I did so, I was pleasantly surprised by the smell of the cool breeze. There was a little hint of jasmine or some other flower in the air, and I was struck by how nice it was to be in that spot at that moment.

And then I realized how frantic I had been feeling just a few minutes ago. The "must make good time and cover many miles" bug had gotten hold of me again, and I had been traveling completely unconsciously.

"Wow," I said to Max. "How nice to get off that highway rat race for a few minutes."

And as we sat eating the meal with the cool, fragrant breeze blowing over us, I knew it was time to stop for the day.

This is an example of how I have learned if I am "on track" or not. Driving mindlessly and endlessly is a very unconscious way to travel. It may get you where you want to go more quickly, but you miss most of the experience of the trip.

When you learn to travel consciously, you stay in the

moment and don't rush yourself.

There really is no reason to rush. It's fine just to put one foot in front of the other and enjoy doing so. And then you can actually enjoy where you are going. Fancy that.

The motorhome has been a great teacher of this lesson for me—it really doesn't lend itself to being rushed anywhere. And because of that, I have learned the value of traveling slowly and mindfully, always.

I highly recommend it.

Five

So after we finish our meal, I take out the Woodall's directory to look for a campground in the area where we can spend the night.

As another sign of how unconsciously I had been traveling, I didn't even know where we were. The Woodall's directory is organized by city, and I had no clue what city we were in.

So I went out into the Target parking lot and asked someone where we were.

Cartersville, they told me, about 30 miles north of Atlanta.

Again, I had to laugh at the wisdom of the angels who were guiding us on our trip.

There was no way that I would have wanted to continue driving with Atlanta so close that we would be getting there at the peak of rush hour. So the angels obviously knew what they were doing when they told me to make that two-mile drive into town rather than getting back on the highway.

Atlanta is tough for anybody to drive through in anything,

let alone a big motorhome being driven by a still pretty inexperienced driver, and during the height of the rush hour.

As I'm counting my blessings for having gotten off the highway when we did, I had a "flashback" to the first time I had driven the motorhome through Atlanta.

The year was 1999, and we had purchased the motorhome that spring. To try it out, Bob and I decided to take it on a trip to Florida.

We had driven down on I-95 but were returning north on I-75. And as we were driving home, I happened to be in the driver's seat when we hit Atlanta—at about 4 pm in afternoon rush hour traffic.

Nothing could have prepared us for that situation: eight lanes of high speed traffic whizzing all around us, and I'm driving—having had about 6 hours of total driving time in my life up to that point.

And I wasn't staying in my lane very well. I wasn't experienced enough to know that a motorhome takes up a lot more space in the lane than a car does. You have to drive it so that the driver's side is much closer to the lane line or you veer into the next lane on the passenger's side.

And I was coming too close to the cars on the passenger side of the motorhome pretty frequently—if the blaring of their horns at me was any indication.

I am sure that the speed of the traffic and the overall stress of the situation contributed to my difficulty. And poor Bob was beside himself since he was sitting in the passenger seat and watching me come close to hitting several cars.

We couldn't do anything but drive through it. There was no way that we could change drivers, and I couldn't manage changing lanes well enough to get off the highway.

But we made it through—again, I'm sure, with the help of a lot of angels—although I didn't have a clue about them back at that point. But I was probably unconsciously sending them a lot of prayers which, thankfully, they heard.

Remembering that time also told me how much I had changed regarding "divine guidance and support."

In 1999, I was just becoming aware of my intuition and was barely learning to trust it.

By 2006, I trusted my intuition completely, and had expanded my consciousness to the point where I was learning to let faith guide my life—not perfectly, but much more of the time.

Our first drive through Atlanta is a story we laugh about today, and, thankfully, it had a happy ending. After more than an hour of driving through that mess, we made it safely out of the Atlanta area and again headed north on I-75.

I was only too happy to take the first available exit and turn the motorhome over to Bob. And I'm sure he was happy to take it over as well.

So as I'm parked just north of Atlanta seven years later, I know enough not to try my luck with that one again, particularly without a person in the passenger seat.

Nope, I think to myself, tomorrow about mid-morning will do just fine for our drive around Atlanta, and we won't be going directly through it this time.

So I look up local campgrounds and find one on a lake just a few exits down the road.

Six

Welcome to Lake Allatoona RV Campground and Marina said the sign as Max and I pulled into their campground a short while later.

Lake Allatoona is a beautiful big lake in the Georgia mountains that provides a lot of the water supply to the Atlanta region.

As we were registering, the office manager suggested that we might want to drive around the campground to check out several available sites. As we did so, we spotted the lake in a more secluded area of the campground.

"Now that is a beautiful spot isn't it Max?" I said to him as we drove the motorhome through that part of the park. "It would be great to stay down here, wouldn't it? You could go swimming right out our front door."

It turned out that the section of the campground near the lake wasn't open because there was still a chance for a freeze, and the water had not been turned on yet. It was just the third week of February, and they normally turned the water on in mid to late March.

But it was so beautiful and peaceful down there that I was happy to live without the water hook-up—I could always use the water in my fresh water tank—if they would just let us camp there.

And they did.

So within an hour, we were hooked up with the main electrical power line, and Max was ready for a swim.

Most Labs love the water and Max is no exception. He loves to swim and Labs are well designed for it: they have webbing between the pads on their feet and a tail that acts like a rotor to propel them through the water.

As we set up camp that night, I thanked God and our travel angels for bringing us to this heavenly spot, and the sunset that night over the lake simply took my breath away it was so beautiful.

And we were visited by a crane that evening—which I took as a special omen since I have always loved that bird.

And it also seemed to indicate that we were on the right path since I had seen another crane on a stop the day before, and you don't see them that often. As it turned out, we saw cranes all along our way on that trip, and I came to think of them as our "bird angels."

Seven

Max and I were the only campers in that whole stretch of the campground, so we were surrounded by the beauty and serenity of the lake, and the stillness of the pine forests.

The next morning we woke up to an absolutely stunning sunrise—I had never seen one so beautiful in my life.

It was so beautiful that I had to get up and grab my camera—even though it was just one of those disposable types—to try and capture it. And we were fortunate enough to be blessed with similar sunrises for most of the mornings that we were there.

It was still cool in the mornings, so we would take a brisk walk around the campground and normally go up and visit the people in the campground office. They had a couple of small dogs that Max had made friends with, and I knew he enjoyed those visits.

By the time we got back from our hike, Max was ready for a swim. Even though the water was cold to me, Max just loved it and jumped in any chance he got.

Since there was no one else around, I would take him off leash and walk him to the edge of the lake. About ten feet away, I would say "OK" and he would go barreling down the rest of the way and make a flying leap into the water.

I quickly learned to stay a good distance back or his flying dive into the water would get me nice and wet as well. His joy was contagious, though, and I couldn't help laughing the whole time we were down there.

He would swim and fetch tennis balls for a good hour before coming up on the bank and stretching out in the spring sun for a rest. And we would just sit there and soak up the beauty of the place.

It was one of the most beautiful places I had ever been, and with the peace and quiet constantly surrounding us, it became one of the most spiritual as well.

Nature is such a good way to connect with the divine. How can you walk in a beautiful grove of trees, or sit by a lovely lake, or do anything out in nature and not be touched by its presence.

I believe that nature does have presence—an energy that is pure and healing. You only have to be open to receiving it.

And after three days of playing with Max in that little bit of heaven, I knew I couldn't leave. I just couldn't stand the thought of leaving that beautiful, private spot only to get back on that crowded, noisy highway.

I knew our time of privacy was not going to last forever. The days and nights were both getting warmer, which meant that they might turn the water on at any time. Plus, other people had seen us camping down there and were thinking about joining us.

So I knew we needed to stay right where we were for as

long as possible. As soon as they turned the water on, we would lose our private retreat.

But until that happened, we planned on enjoying every moment.

Eight

And as the days became weeks, I began to feel like that was why we had been brought to this lovely place—for me to be surrounded by the divine presence in nature and heal.

Heal my body, heal my heart, and heal the part of me that was still not willing to make a firm commitment to a path of "thy will be done."

I had been working on this commitment for many years, and all of my earlier quests had helped move me along this path. But I was still resisting making that full commitment.

Some part of me was still too afraid to relinquish control, and I would find myself slipping back into the "it's my life and I'm in charge of it" mindset.

The very idea of even wanting to make such a commitment may sound strange to you.

But I have come to believe that it is a natural part of a spiritual journey: you just come to realize that God, or the divine, or whatever you want to call that higher power, knows more than you do, and the idea of letting that "greater consciousness" lead you becomes more and more attractive.

The real motivation was the peace that such a choice brought into my life. Out went the stress, the worry, the aggravation—everything that created discord and disharmony was released.

And in its place was a true sense of gratitude, contentment

and inner peace. And the more I experienced little bits of this type of inner peace, the more I wanted it to continue.

It's not something that is easy to explain—you really have to experience it for yourself. But it is a place that I believe we all can live if we can just learn how to do so.

And a big step for me was to learn to listen to myself, and to take responsibility for my own life. I have learned that the divine resides inside of us—we are a part of the divine. And as we reclaim that divine essence inside of ourselves, we open the channel for divine guidance to enter our lives.

That is what I felt I was there to do—but, again, I was experiencing some form of resistance that was keeping me trapped in the old way of thinking.

In my journals from that time, I asked myself why I was continuing to block this process, and this was what my resistance had to say:

"Being connected to the divine will be no fun—no wine, no TV, no nothing—except inner peace of course. Being connected to the divine will require me to be perfect—which I will never be because I am human—so why try? Being connected to the divine will be lonely—how many other people think like that? Not very many, and since regular people don't understand my choices, they will think that I'm either nuts or stupid or both—and that will lead to a lot of rejection."

So I began to understand the barriers I was still facing on my journey to consciousness: I thought it would be no fun, I thought I had to be perfect, and I thought I would experience a lot of rejection.

None of the above was correct, but I didn't know it at the time.

That was what I thought and it was holding me back from

making a full commitment to living a conscious life. But I also journaled how I had changed:

"I am no longer afraid of living alone. I am no longer afraid of dying. I am no longer afraid of not having enough money. I am no longer afraid to speak my truth. I am no longer afraid to displease other people."

This told me how much I had changed during the decade or so of this process. Those were significant changes and I felt very grounded in making those statements.

But I also realized that there were still things that I was afraid of, like:

"I am still afraid to drive and use the motorhome--getting better at it but it still scares me. I am afraid of Max's strength and his "surprise" uncontrollability--I know how strong he has become. I am afraid that I will be fat forever. I am afraid that I don't know how to support myself financially and also walk the path of a conscious life."

So that was my state of mind in March of 2006. I would describe it as half way in and half way out. I had made a lot of progress on my path towards consciousness, but I clearly still had a long way to go.

And my prayer for help in moving me forward on my path towards consciousness was answered in a most surprising way: I broke my leg.

Nine

Yup, broke my leg—my left leg just below the knee joint.

Max and I had been happily settled down by the lake for the last few weeks. We had a nice routine of morning walks, swimming, lunch, my reading/his napping, more swimming, dinner, and then early to bed.

We were enjoying ourselves thoroughly.

And I was feeling a great sense of peace and healing in that very beautiful and spiritual spot. And I really felt like I was making progress on my desire to heal my body, my heart, and make a full commitment to a conscious way of life.

And I had been paying special attention to my body—I had brought along exercise tapes and had been using them daily.

My body was a big issue for me: I was sick and tired of the thirty extra pounds that I had gained over the last decade. But I was also trying to move past the "beating myself up over it" stage and on to a more positive and healthy path.

In my journaling, I was reminded that I had lived a fairly athletic life-style for most of my life: my family was very active in sports, including snow skiing, water skiing, and golf. I had even earned a letter in high school varsity tennis.

More recently, I had ridden in four of our local annual "Pedal to the Point" bike marathons (150 mile 2-day rides) to raise money for Multiple Sclerosis research. And I had taken up country line dancing and had been enjoying that for several years.

Maybe it was because I was always so active and in pretty good shape that this period of being over-weight was bothering me so much.

But I also had to be honest enough with myself to recognize that my eating and drinking habits had deteriorated—I was pretty much sacrificing my body to cope with this consciousness process. I had been going through a really rough time trying to excavate all that emotional debris from the past, and I had learned to turn to my "TV/comfort food/wine routine" to cope with it all.

But I knew that I would never live the kind of conscious life that I was seeking if I continued to neglect my physical health. And being in that beautiful, peaceful place allowed me to finally find the motivation to begin to treat my body with more respect.

And I thought that I could do it on my own—I had been diligent about using the exercise tapes, and was beginning to see some results.

But, once again, the universe must have been listening to my prayers to have something "help me break out of these negative health patterns."

I didn't know that it would materialize as a broken leg, but the injury did help me move along on that path. And maybe it took something of that magnitude to knock me out of that negative orbit.

And this is how it all happened.

Ten

Since I wasn't towing a car, we had to take the motorhome into Cartersville about once a week to stock up on groceries and refill the fresh water tank.

On Monday, March 6, 2006, we made just such a trip. We always went into town early in the morning so that the motorhome would still be cool for Max while I went in and did the shopping.

When we got back to the campground later that day, I noticed that our firewood and the long leash that I used for Max near our picnic table were both gone. I didn't worry about it too much because I assumed that the maintenance crew in the campground might have cleaned up the site thinking that we had left.

So we had a snack, took a swim, and enjoyed the rest of the warm, sunny day.

The next morning, I asked about the wood and leash when we made our daily visit to the campground office. The manager called the maintenance crew and the security guard, but no one knew anything about the wood or the leash.

So I told the manager that it was no big deal—we would be fine without them. I hadn't made any fires anyway because it had been so cool in the evenings that we preferred to be inside, and I had another tie-out line that would work for Max.

But later that night—after a nice day of swimming, walking, etc.—Max and I were startled by the roar of a car into our campsite. Max, who had been sleeping at the time, jumped up and started barking to beat the band.

"Quiet big boy, let me see what's going on," I told him.

Since it was dusk, it was hard to see who was out there and I got a little nervous—which Max probably sensed.

After a few minutes, I thought I recognized the security guard's car. I had seen the car circle through our area once or twice at night while we were camped there, and Max and I had finally met him on one of our evening walks.

"It's OK, Max, it's just the security guard. Let's go see what he wants." I figured I'd take Max out to say hello and take care of his last potty stop for the night.

After I had put on Max's collar and slipped the leash over my left wrist, I opened the door to let us outside. I had taught Max to wait and come out after me so that we wouldn't run the risk of accidents while going down the motorhome steps.

But that night he took off through the door like he had been shot out of a cannon. And I went out right behind him because the leash was around my wrist.

In the blink of an eye, I'm on the ground and cannot get up.

"Are you hurt?" asks the security guard.

"I'm not sure, but I think so. I feel sort of dazed so I think I'll just sit here for a moment," I responded.

It didn't take very long before we both knew that I was not going to get up. I was sitting a good eight feet from the motorhome and I hadn't touched a step on the way out. Max must have taken a flying leap out of the door and I went right behind him.

It was like a clumsy broad jump, only I landed so hard that the two bones in my left leg collided and the lower one, the tibia, got chipped near the knee joint.

I didn't know all this at the time of the accident, of course. I had no idea that I was injured as seriously as I was. But I was pretty dizzy and my leg was beginning to ache.

I have taken spills before in my life and normally bounced back pretty well. So sitting there on the ground, I figured I had pulled a muscle or something and I would be back up and running in no time.

But since I couldn't get up, the security guard felt it would be best to call 911 and get me seen by a doctor that night.

Max, meanwhile, was having a gay old time running around with his leash in his mouth, oblivious to the situation. After I called to him, he came over and started licking me with a curious look on his face like "why are you still on the ground?"

The security guard took Max over to a nearby clump of trees so he could do his business, and then he put Max back in the motorhome while we waited for the EMS people to arrive.

The security guard had also called the campground manager who came down in her car to check out the situation. She retrieved my purse from the motorhome and told me that she would check on Max while I was gone.

The EMS ambulance arrived and the kind gentlemen bundled me up in a big leg brace and loaded me into the vehicle.

Max was not happy with this turn of events if his barking was any indication. I suspect that he sensed the tension around the situation and just didn't like the idea of me going somewhere without him.

"I'll be back, Max, just rest and wait for me," I had told him before being put in the ambulance.

So off we went to the emergency room in Cartersville. By this time, I was in quite a bit of pain, and beginning to get worried that something a little more serious had happened than I had first thought.

Eleven

Three hours later, I am on my way back to the campground. The security guard had been kind enough to drive up and get me once they had released me from the emergency room.

The emergency room doctor had ordered several x-rays, and had told me that I had a small fracture in my lower leg. He gave me a prescription for pain pills, and put a brace on my leg that would not allow it to bend.

"You need to see an orthopedic surgeon as soon as possible," he advised, and gave me the name of one in the area.

So there I was, in a wheelchair with my leg straight out in front of me, and still in a lot of pain since I had only had a bag of ice on it since I had gotten there.

It was a long night—but it would have been a lot longer and much more difficult if I hadn't had the help of the campground personnel.

The campground manager was very sympathetic and wanted to do whatever she could to help us given the situation. She gave the security guard permission to help me and he was nice enough to take me in to see the orthopedic surgeon several days later.

The accident had happened on a Tuesday night and I wasn't able to see a doctor until the next Monday afternoon.

And it was a long and difficult week in between.

I had gotten a pair of crutches at the hospital so I could move around the motorhome somewhat. The emergency room doctor had told me that I shouldn't put any weight at all on my leg, so I didn't.

Fortunately, we had plenty of food because of our shopping trip the day before. But I could no longer walk Max and he obviously needed to be taken out on a regular basis.

I also hadn't been able to fill the prescription for the pain pills, and there was a constant pain in the back of my knee.

"We're in kind of a mess, now aren't we," I confided to Max the next day. I still didn't have a clear notion of what was really wrong with my leg, and was assuming that my leg would heal with proper rest and enough time.

That was what I expected the doctor to tell me, and that first week I assumed that I just needed to stay off it and I'd be doing the right thing for it to begin to heal.

I managed Max by letting him out in the mornings off leash. Again I thanked the heavens for guiding me to give him this training. What could I possibly have done if he wasn't under voice control?

He didn't want to leave me and go out on his own at first, but I knew it wouldn't be wise for me to try and walk over that rocky ground on crutches. What we didn't need was me taking another fall.

So he eventually figured out that I wasn't coming and that he could go on his own. He would come back when I called and that routine worked most of the time.

Once or twice I lost sight of him behind some trees when he was down by the water, and he took a quick dip in the lake before I could call to him—which was actually OK with me given the circumstances.

Since I knew he still needed some vigorous exercise every day, I managed to drag myself over to our favorite swimming spot in the afternoon.

It was the one spot where he could get in and out of the lake on sand, and that was much better on his paws as he ran in and out of the water to retrieve the balls.

So we muddled through as best as we could. Max was a real trooper. And I did my best to keep a positive attitude about the whole thing.

But I still had to figure out how I was ever going to get us home since I couldn't get behind the wheel of the motorhome with my leg in this big cast.

But getting home, as it turned out, was not going to be in the cards for several months to come.

Twelve

The orthopedic surgeon that I finally got in to see gave me the bad news: my injured leg would require surgery if it was ever going to be fully functional again.

He recommended that I have the surgery right away since delaying it raised the risk that the broken chip of bone might move around and then not be operable. He could schedule it for next week.

But how, I thought to myself, am I going to take care of Max while I'm in for surgery and then afterwards. The doctor had said that it would take me several weeks on crutches to recover and then quite a bit of physical therapy.

It was then that I began to realize the true depth of the predicament that we were in—and, I must confess, I began to feel pretty scared.

"Here I am alone, and what in heaven's name am I going to do now?" I thought to myself.

But as overwhelming as the situation seemed, somehow I also had faith that everything would work out OK.

Our couple of weeks in that "little bit of heaven" apparently had a big affect on me—I just had a strong sense of faith that I could figure it out and that the angels would be there to help me.

I had journaled on the morning of the day of the accident that "my job here is to become mentally, emotionally and physically strong enough in my core to withstand anything and still hold my center. That is why I am in this magical place—my little bit of heaven on earth—to help me gain that strength. And it is an aware strength—an observant, patient, listening, empathic strength. I don't react to the world, to the happenings in my life—I just observe them, with total acceptance for exactly what is at that particular moment in time."

Accepting what is. That is a biggie. My journal entry showed me that I had gotten the message intellectually. My broken leg was going to anchor that message in my heart.

Thirteen

I called my kids to let them know what had happened, and both of them offered to fly out and help. My daughter, Jennifer, was living and working in Portland, Oregon, and my son, William, was in law school in Cleveland, Ohio, so neither were anywhere close by.

Plus, the weather in Mentor was still very wintry so driving the motorhome back up north wasn't looking like a very good option in any case.

I had also called Maureen and told her the news. She offered to help in any way she could, but I couldn't see how being at the Outer Banks would work either.

And then I thought of my friend Bob, who you first met in Part One. He was still living in Florida, about a day's drive away, but we hadn't really been in communication with each other for over a year. And it didn't seem fair to ask this of him after all of that time.

But I knew of all of my possible options, he was the best. He knew and liked Max, and could handle him. Not everybody can, given Max's size. He also knew how to drive the motorhome and he wasn't that far away. And, given that it was March, Florida would be a better place to recuperate than Ohio.

So I called him. And he was the great friend and gentleman that he's always been. I explained the situation as best as I understood it, and he asked me what he could do to help. He offered to drive up to the campground, and then drive us and the motorhome back with his truck in tow.

I explained that it might take a month or so for my leg to heal (not yet understanding that it was actually going to take me three or four months just to get off the crutches), and would it be OK with Randy and Nancy, the owners of the Quail Roost RV Campground, for us to stay that long? And, did they even have a vacant place for us to park?

Bob said that he would check with them, and let me know. He called back the next day to say that it was fine with them and that they could find a place for us to park.

Meanwhile, the security guard at the campground had offered to drive us to Quail Roost to save Bob the drive up. I offered to pay him for his time and gas if the campground manager would give him permission to take us there.

Which she did. So within a few days, we had worked out a plan where the security guard would drive us and the motorhome to Florida, and tow his truck so he would have it to drive back to Georgia.

Fourteen

We arrived safely at Quail Roost on March 15th, eight days after the accident. We had left at 5 am that morning to beat the Atlanta traffic, and I just had to laugh to myself as we drove through that metropolis.

I was sitting in the seat across from Max with my leg propped up on a crutch resting on the sofa.

"Not exactly the way we had planned it, is it Maxie?"

It was becoming a very big lesson that we cannot always "control" our lives or what life will bring. The accident was just that: an accident. I hadn't expected anything like this to happen to me, but it had. And now it was up to me on how I was going to respond to it.

That's an important distinction, I believe. We don't always have control over what happens in our life, but we do have control over our response to it. And that choice of how we respond is very important.

We can choose to respond as a victim and live a life filled with self-pity or worse.

Or we can choose to accept what life brings us and deal with it as best as we can. And we can even bring a positive and grateful attitude to the situation.

I chose the latter. Or I chose it as often as I was able.

Yes, I was in a mess. Yes, I was burdening Bob with both my and Max's care for several months. Yes, I was going to need an operation and I didn't have a doctor that I knew and trusted. Yes, it was going to be expensive and I was going to be unemployed for several months.

Yes, all of that was true and wasn't easy to accept.

But I had learned by that time that "resisting what is" doesn't work either.

Resisting what is just causes more pain, because in addition to what you had to go through, you are also burdening yourself and everyone else with all that additional emotional stress.

The "poor me" mentality is very tiring—for everyone involved.

So that wasn't going to be my choice. I was going to make a concerted effort to accept what was happening with as much grace and good humor as I could.

And I feel like I did a pretty good job of staying that course. And so did Bob and Max.

Not that it was easy, for any of us.

Fifteen

Bob was a real hero. He took me to endless doctor's appointments, to the grocery store on a regular basis, and everywhere else I needed to go—crutches and all.

He had a two-door truck at the time, and he had to put the crutches in either the narrow little space behind the seats or open the truck bed cover every time he took me some place. It was a constant process of crutches in, crutches, out, crutches in, crutches out—many times during each trip we took.

I'm sure at some point he would have liked to have just given those stupid crutches a good "heave ho" and never touched them again.

But he never complained and really displayed a great deal of patience throughout the whole ordeal.

And it was an ordeal.

First, I had to find a doctor. That took me a week.

Then I had to schedule an appointment—that took another week.

Then the surgery had to be scheduled, but not until the pre-operative tests were completed, including an EKG on my heart, an MRI on my leg, and several blood tests to determine if I could undergo the surgery.

My accident occurred on March 7th, and the soonest I could do the surgery was April 10th.

And my recovery time on crutches was another three months, and then I graduated to a walker, and then a cane—for a total of about five months of being unable to walk normally. Actually six months from the date of the accident.

And then there was the surgery itself.

The doctor had told us that the surgery could be done on an out-patient basis but that he would reserve a hospital room just in case.

But what was supposed to be a possible one night stay, ended up being three. And it would have been longer if I hadn't managed to escape.

What a nightmare.

Sixteen

After considering several ways to get the surgery done, Bob and I had decided that I would go down for the surgery (the hospital was about 40 miles south of us, near Tampa) while he stayed at Quail Roost and took care of Max. That seemed the easiest for everyone considering what the doctor had told us.

So I arranged for transportation to get me down and back because the doctor told me not to try and drive myself home right after the surgery.

Going down there on my own did not prove to be a great decision. It left me without an advocate for my care, and I believe that I suffered because of it.

I'm not sure to this day just what went wrong since I was under general anesthesia for the surgery and a good while afterwards.

What I do know is that my surgery was scheduled for 11 am that morning and it happened about noon. Fine.

I was told that the surgery would take about three hours and I guess it did.

After surgery, I was rolled into a waiting area to recover from the anesthesia and wait until a hospital room was available. No one ever asked me if I wanted to stay in the hospital, but it was very clear to me that I wasn't in any shape to go anywhere.

I was to call my driver when I was ready to go home, and if he didn't hear from me, he would check with me the next day.

I was in no shape to call anybody—and that is when I really needed someone with me as it turned out.

Again, I don't really know what happened and my questions later to the doctor and the nurses didn't give me any good answers. But I do know that I was in that recovery area until 11 pm that night—and I think I was the last patient to leave even though I was in the morning surgery round.

I finally got taken to a hospital room about 11:30 pm— and then the real fun started.

The nurses apparently changed shifts about that time and I remember a new set of faces coming in to check on me about midnight or so. Why hospitals think it's helpful to keep waking patients up all night long is beyond me, but that is what they did.

At some point, I told the nurse that my injured leg felt hot—they had a wrap on my leg that included an ice water system that had been keeping it cold before.

So she brought in a big bag of ice and laid it next to my leg.

Not too much later, I told her it didn't seem to be helping—and got nowhere with it.

The nurses changed shifts again early the next morning and when that nurse came in she took one look at my situation and swore under her breath.

"What the heck is going on here?" she said.

It turned out that the ice was suppose to be put in the little cooler on the floor that had a tube attached to the wrap on my leg. That is how the water in my wrap stayed cold. They just had to keep the cooler filled with ice water.

No wonder it hadn't helped when the other nurse had put the bag of ice on the outside of my leg. The wrap on my leg was insulated and the ice couldn't penetrate through it.

Seventeen

Let's just say that this was an example of the care that I received that first night and I was exhausted and in a lot of pain by the next morning—apparently I also wasn't given enough pain medication during the night.

I was scheduled to be released that day, but I couldn't even get to the bathroom on my own so how was I going to be able to handle a 40 mile ride home in a bumpy car and then live in a motorhome for the next few weeks?

The nurse on duty that day told all this to the doctor, but he still wanted me to go. I knew I was in no shape to go anywhere and the nurse agreed. She finally convinced him that I should stay another day and I did receive better care that night.

I had gone in for surgery on Monday morning, and felt OK to go by Wednesday morning, but by then they didn't want to let me go.

It went from them wanting to push me out the door on Tuesday morning to not wanting me to go until Friday.

One of the most frustrating things about that time was the lack of what I felt was real information—I just couldn't get straight answers to any of my questions—if I could even find anyone to ask.

It appeared that they were now very concerned about my recovery if I went home to the motorhome. How was I going to get to physical therapy? How was I going to get up and down the stairs on crutches without falling? How was I going to cook and care for my basic needs in a motorhome?

Of course, they didn't ask me any of these questions directly or I could have told them that I had been handling these very issues for over a month.

They had decided—they being a vague "somebody" in charge of my release—that I needed to stay in the hospital until an assisted care bed opened up and then I should stay there for another week or so.

I knew I wasn't in great shape—I was still in a lot of pain and weak from the whole ordeal—but I wasn't getting better staying there with them waking me up every time I finally fell into a good sleep. I doubt that I slept longer than two hours at a time during those three days.

After a frustrating Tuesday, I woke up Wednesday morning determined to get out of that ridiculous situation. So I used my cell phone to find hotels in the area—thinking that if I could get that far, at least I could get a good night's sleep and start to recover.

I called Bob to see how things were going with him and Max, and he told me that they were fine and enjoying their "guy time together"—chips and chicken wings while watching the sports shows, etc.

He was concerned about my situation and offered to come and get me—even drive the motorhome down if that would make the trip back more comfortable for me.

But I was worried about my leg. It just didn't feel right, and I thought I should stay a little closer to the hospital and the doctor's office in case an infection set in. I didn't want Bob to make all that effort on Wednesday, only to have to bring me back a few days later.

So we decided that I would try and get out of the hospital, but stay close by until Friday or Saturday. I had called my driver and it would work for him to pick me up on either of those days.

So I ended up making a reservation at a nearby hotel that had a handicapped room available. Now I just had to get there.

I had actually been officially released on Monday so I could leave if I could figure out how to get myself and my stuff out the door.

To protect the innocent, let's just say that I was able to "find" a wheelchair and get to the front door of the hospital.

I was able to take the hotel courtesy van over to it—although I had to get in and out of it by going up and down on my bottom since I couldn't manage steps on my crutches.

But I had gotten used to that access method since it was what I had been doing to get in and out of the motorhome ever since the accident. It was ungraceful to say the least, but it worked.

So I made my escape and prayed for the strength to see this through on my own.

I felt foolish needing to leave like that, but it had become clear that other people were making decisions about my life that I needed to be making. I had to take back responsibility for my own care and my own life.

Things got a lot better once I was at the hotel. They had a small wheelchair that I could use and the handicapped room was set up to accommodate my condition pretty well.

All I wanted to do was sleep in any case. "Just give me a clean bed and a quiet room" I kept thinking to myself.

I checked into the hotel on Wednesday afternoon, and by the time I left that next Saturday, I was feeling a lot better.

When I had first gotten to the hotel, I had felt pretty alone and pretty depressed—I even needed to have a good cry or two. But over the three days that I was there, I started to feel my inner strength returning—and it seemed to be returning at a deeper and stronger level.

I began to realize that experiences like the one I was having can stretch a person if one allows that to happen. I was able to see my circumstances as a challenge, but a challenge that I could handle—with the help of my angels of course.

And while I did have a few low points where I wished that someone was there to take care of me, I somehow knew that I could do it on my own—and that I wasn't really alone—that the divine was right there with me if I just opened my heart to it.

So bit by bit—task by tiring task—I regained my strength.

Three days does not seem like a long time, but it was long

enough for me to learn endurance, patience, and a much deeper commitment to the divine. I drew frequently on the time I had spent at Lake Allatoona, and couldn't help but remember that my task was to develop this type of inner strength.

It's not an experience that I would wish on anyone else, but it worked for me.

With my strength beginning to return, I was more than ready to go home. The driver picked me up on Saturday morning and we were back at Quail Roost about two hours later.

Yes I was tired when we got back, but the hugs from Bob and the many licks from Max began to make my world feel right again. I was really glad to be home.

Eighteen

The next two months were devoted to trying to get my knee to bend.

Which it wasn't.

I had chosen a doctor near Tampa because I originally thought he was connected to my hospital up north, and I wanted someone I could trust.

I was not very comfortable with the idea of surgery in the first place. I just didn't like the idea of someone cutting into me I guess. But once I realized I really had no choice about the surgery, I set about trying to get the best doctor I could find.

About a hundred phone calls later and I finally decided on the doctor near Tampa. I didn't realize at the time that it wouldn't be a very convenient choice either for the surgery or the physical therapy which was to follow.

The whole situation had turned out to be a much bigger

ordeal than I could have possibly imagined.

In any case, once I was back at Quail Roost, I needed to start to work my knee and leg to get it functional again. And I was having a lot of trouble getting it to work.

This is just speculation, but I often wonder if my mind wasn't playing a role in the process at that point. I had been warned—strongly warned—right after the accident occurred not to bend my knee in any way or the bone chip might move and I couldn't have the surgery.

I think that really scared me—actually, I know it did.

So for the four weeks between the accident and the surgery, I had to keep telling myself not to bend my knee. And it was even harder because it was in a soft brace not a cast, and I had to hold it stiff—constantly.

After that much time of telling myself not to bend it or else, I probably shouldn't have been surprised that it wouldn't bend easily after the surgery.

I wondered if I didn't have a mental block still in place. And maybe an emotional one from fear as well?

I asked my doctor and physical therapist if this could be the case, but only got some looks like "let's just pretend you didn't just ask those questions," so I let it go. But I should have listened to myself.

But, at that point, I was still weak and tired and just wanted my knee to get better. So I enrolled in the physical therapy program recommended by my doctor and made the sixty mile trip every week to work on it their way. And I did all the exercises that they gave me and did them very conscientiously.

But I wasn't making much progress.

And certainly not as much as my doctor expected—which he was only too happy to tell me on my check-ups. So after two months of this treatment, I began to lose faith in the whole situation and just wanted to go home. Every visit was just a little bit more demoralizing—and I was paying for it!

I actually felt like I made more progress in the swimming pool at Quail Roost, which I could finally use about a month after the operation when the risk of infection had passed. The water felt so refreshing and I felt much more connected to my leg—like we were a team again instead of it being a distant appendage.

By the end of May, Bob was ready to head north to visit his mother and brother for a few months, and Max and I were more than ready to go with him.

Nineteen

While I was still on crutches and wouldn't be able to put any weight on my left leg for another month or so, we felt we could manage driving back to Ohio in tandem.

Bob would drive his truck and pull his trailer with his motorcycle on it as he had originally planned. I couldn't drive the truck because it was a stick shift and I couldn't use my left leg.

And I would drive the motorhome with Max on board.

We felt it would be safer and easier for me if we went together, and it undoubtedly was. Bob did all the gas fill-ups for both vehicles, which saved me from trying to do it on crutches.

I could bend my leg enough to get behind the wheel of the motorhome, but I still couldn't put any weight on it. This made for an interesting "balancing act" just getting in and out of the driver's seat since it was a step off the floor of the motorhome. And the fewer times I had to get in and out of the seat the better—neither of us had the strength to handle another fall.

So as we packed up to begin our trip north, I reflected on what this experience had taught me.

Yes, it had been an ordeal. Most of the last three months had been taken up with handling the "accident" of the broken leg, and it had not been a fun experience.

But it had also taught me a great deal. It had taught me patience. I had to be very patient with myself, with Max, with Bob, and with everyone else and everything else that I encountered. What good would it have done to be otherwise? It would only have made everything that much harder—on everyone.

I had learned endurance. I had endured a great deal in the hospital, in the hotel, and then back in the motorhome. I had endured a lot of pain, a lot of frustration, a lot of fear, a lot of loneliness, and even some self-pity on occasion. But I had always tried to endure it with grace—and that had created more grace in my life.

And I had learned to trust myself and to trust in my own strength. The time at the hotel and having only myself to rely on strengthened that trust a great deal. It felt like I grew up emotionally—I had no choice but to take responsibility for my own care, as difficult as it was in that situation.

And Max had been great through it all—he would gently lick me and come over whenever he could to let me rub his soft ears. He was a gentle giant and he really kept my spirits up when they could so easily have fallen. I'm not sure how I could have managed without him and Bob, and I will forever feel very grateful for them both.

So, yes the accident was an ordeal. But it was also a very big gift.

Twenty

Several years earlier, Bob and I had discovered Tunica, Mississippi—the home of about ten large casinos. A mini Las Vegas if you will. And while we are not big gamblers, we did enjoy the buffets and the excitement of it all.

A few of the casinos there have very nice motorhome parks and they charge a very reasonable rate—and they are dog friendly.

I thought it would be a nice idea to go home by taking a little side trip over to Tunica. And it would be a good way to thank Bob for three very challenging months of caring for Max and me.

So just after the Memorial Day weekend, we started our journey north to Tunica before heading to Ohio. We stopped at an RV park the first night on the trip, and arrived in Tunica later in the afternoon of the second day.

It was a fun but also challenging next few days.

The Sam's Town RV park where we stayed was very nice and we ended up with a large site that worked well for walking Max. There was also plenty of room for both the motorhome and Bob's truck and motorcycle trailer.

But when we had planned the trip, I really hadn't thought about how I would get around in the casinos. I was still on crutches and that is a very tough way to walk for any distance. It just wears out your arms and your one good leg pretty quickly.

I really didn't want to complain that my arms were getting tired and ruin Bob's good time, so I just toughed it out—at least for the first day. We had asked if they had any wheelchairs and were told no.

But we asked again on the second day and they found one for us—so now Bob had the job of pushing me around the casinos. Because the casinos were so crowded, the going was very slow and I didn't help matters with my constant "go this way, no go that way" directions.

At one buffet, I thought sure that I was going to be swimming with the goldfish that were in a pond under the bridge that we were passing over. I had asked him one too many times to reverse directions so I could see some different food.

I must say that I will never take my mobility for granted again. And I have gained tremendous respect for people who have mobility limitations. It was so hard getting around in a wheelchair—and the world is just not built to accommodate them either.

That buffet was a good example of this point: I couldn't see any of the food unless I raised myself up on the arm rests of the chair. The buffet displays were built too high for me to see anything. I'm sure they were designed for the comfort of people walking past, but that didn't help anyone in a wheelchair.

And poor Bob had to put up with all this for me to get my food at the buffet, and then he had to go back through the line again for himself.

A hero, I tell you, a hero.

Twenty-One

After a somewhat enjoyable visit to Tunica, we again headed north to Ohio.

Bob's family lives in Elyria, Ohio, which is about 70 miles

west of Mentor. He had planned to travel with us back to Mentor, help us get set-up for a few days, and then go over to visit his mother and brother.

My daughter, Jennifer, was coming for a visit to help me after he headed over to Elyria. And my son, Will, would be there to help as well.

So all in all, I was being very well cared for, and I felt very grateful.

Max was not quite so fortunate.

Ever since the accident, Max had been getting the short end of the stick—at least from me. I just hadn't been able to give him the same kind of loving attention that I had been giving to him before.

I couldn't exercise him as often, and I couldn't even sit next to him for fear of further injuring my leg. And he wasn't allowed up on the bed anymore for the same reason.

Bob did a lot for Max while we were at Quail Roost, including taking him on daily morning and evening walks. But he also had other commitments for his time since he helped out with the maintenance of the Quail Roost campground.

And Max hated my crutches—which I couldn't really blame him for given that I had dropped one or both near him on several occasions. And while the crutches didn't actually fall on him, they made a lot of noise and he had to jump out of the way.

And I really feel that Max sensed the physical and emotional challenges that I was going through. Dogs are so sensitive to our moods and emotions that I don't see how it could have been otherwise.

So while Max had his basic needs met while we were in Florida, he wasn't living the same quality of life that he had been before the accident.

And I was determined to give that back to him as soon as I possibly could.

And getting back home to Mentor was a good first step.

I am sure that he was thrilled to finally get out of the motorhome, and back to his own bed—and that he had more than two feet of space in which to turn around.

Max has always been a good sport about everything, but living with me in such cramped quarters for so long—and with me using the crutches and walker on top of it—must have been a very stressful time for him.

So now we needed to get our life put back together.

Twenty-Two

Since I was still on crutches, I knew that I needed to find someone else to walk Max on a regular basis. He needed more exercise than I could give him, and I was determined to make that happen.

So I called Jane Babisnsky, our favorite dog trainer. Jane had taught the dog training class at PetSmart that we had attended in the fall of 2004, and was also our TDI trainer and tester. So I asked her if she knew of anyone who could help us out.

And she did—she told me about her friend Lynn Way who helped her with training dogs on occasion. Lynn also lived near us so it would be convenient for her as well.

I called Lynn and asked her to come over to meet Max. Jane's recommendation meant a lot to me, and I knew it was going to be really hard to find someone who could handle such a big dog.

Lynn and Max hit it off right away. She had handled big dogs before and wasn't at all intimidated by his size.

So off they went for his first long walk around the neighborhood in four months. Lynn reported that he did great on the walk, and that she would really enjoy walking him on a regular basis.

After working out a very reasonable payment plan, Lynn agreed to walk Max three times a week for the next several months. I knew that it would take me time to get back to walking him for any long distance, and this would be a great way to give him the exercise he needed during my recovery.

I felt a great sense of relief when Lynn left. I knew that vigorous exercise would be a great help in relieving the stress that he had experienced while we were in Florida.

While I couldn't walk him, I realized that I still wanted to be part of his active life. Being active together had been a big part of our bonding experience, and I didn't want to lose it completely.

So I decided to explore places where I could take him swimming. With summer upon us, nothing would be more fun than for him to cool off in a local pond or our own fresh water lake—Lake Erie. I had looked for places for him to swim the summer before, and had found a few good spots.

One was a local park that had a nice beach on the Lake where he could get in and swim. The problem was that it was about a mile walk to get to the beach—which was obviously not an option for me at that point.

The park also had a marina, which was another way to get to the Lake, but you needed an access code to get into that area—which, of course, I didn't have.

So one hot day I decided to just drive over there and hope that the gate to the marina would be open so Max and I could drive through and get to the Lake.

The gate was closed. But there was a guard in the guardhouse who agreed to let us though after I explained my situation.

And, yes, I felt very grateful to the "dog angels" for helping us out. I'm sure that they realized that Max needed to swim and they probably whispered in the guard's ear that it would be OK. He didn't look like someone who would normally be so agreeable, but I delighted that he had said yes.

So Max had a great time that day retrieving tennis balls and frisbees from the water. It truly was a healing day for both of us.

The sun was hot, the sky was blue, and the water refreshingly cool.

I couldn't throw the balls and frisbees very well on my crutches, but Max didn't seem to mind. He just loved being in the water and running free along the beach.

It was the first time since we had returned to Mentor that I actually felt relaxed and at peace about Max, and began to feel that things would be OK.

Nature has a way of "smoothing my feathers" like nothing else I have ever found.

After that experience, I redoubled my efforts to find a place where I could take Max to the Lake on a regular basis. And finally all my searching paid off: we found a spot just outside the boundary of a state park where I could take him.

Needless to say, we spent many a happy day down there

that summer, and I thanked the heavens for helping us to find it.

It was a healing place and time for both of us.

Twenty-Three

During the following months, I slowly regained my mobility and continued to work on getting my knee to bend.

I had gone to see a local orthopedic surgeon soon after I returned to Mentor so that I would have local medical care, and to get started on more physical therapy.

The doctor had taken x-rays and said that everything looked fine, and referred me to the physical therapy clinic next door. The physical therapist took me right away and we began working on some new exercises.

But it didn't seem to be working.

I would go to my appointments and do the exercises both there and at home. But my knee was still not bending very well. And given my experience with the physical therapy process in Florida, I was really beginning to have my doubts that my knee would ever be OK again.

This became apparent when I tried to plant some flowers in the garden later that summer. I couldn't get down on my knees to do it, so I just had to bend over in an awkward position to put the plants in the ground.

And that would not do.

Gardening had been an avid interest of mine for a long time, and I had found it especially healing since I had moved to Mentor.

When I moved to the condo with Max in the summer of 2004, the front yard landscaping was quite over-grown and pretty scraggly looking. I didn't do much with it that first summer because we were busy getting settled inside, and I wasn't sure what I could do since I was only renting the property.

But by that next spring, I had felt a real push to get out there and get my hands in the dirt. I hadn't done any gardening since selling my house four years earlier, and I really had missed it.

So, after agreeing with my nice landlords, Joanne and Jim, to share the expense of the project, I completely relandscaped the front and side gardens.

I had carefully made up a gardening plan that would not require much maintenance after I left. Since it was a rental property, I didn't want to create a lot of work for the next tenants or any problems for Joanne and Jim.

Bob came over a couple of times during the summer and helped me take out several large bushes. By the time we were finished, we had created a very nice new yard. It even won the "best new landscaping" prize from the Village Greene Condo Association that year.

This was done, of course, in the summer of 2005—a year before my accident and when I had full use of both of my legs.

The summer of 2006 was a different matter. And it really struck home that I was still disabled when I couldn't get out there and take care of the yard like I had the year before.

My daughter, Jenny, had helped me put down several bags of mulch when she was there in June, and that had really helped a lot. But there was still a lot more that I wanted to do.

"Good thing that we made this a low maintenance yard,"

I thought to myself as I surveyed the situation.

But I felt sad that I wasn't able to get down on my knees and work in the dirt like I wanted to. I could get down and sit on the ground, but I couldn't get back up without looking very silly with my one stiff knee.

My difficulty in gardening motivated me to look for other solutions to the healing of my leg. If the physical therapy wasn't working, I'd just have to find something that would.

Twenty-Four

I was fortunate enough to find a wonderful massage/ physical therapist while glancing through the Mentor recreation brochure for the fall. David Hansen, who is a licensed massage therapist, practices a form of holistic therapeutic massage that focuses on enhancing wellness in the entire body.

I knew that I was on the right track from the moment I met him. David is so kind and so gentle, and yet quite effective in working with the energy in the body. He specializes in helping people who have injured their body or who are experiencing chronic pain.

I have long believed in the holistic approach to body care. I have read a lot about the mind-body connection, and am absolutely convinced that we are one large energy system.

Everything was connected in the body; that was something David and I both believed in, and I just knew that I needed to have that approach if I was to truly heal my injured leg.

The physical therapy had been fine, but it wasn't a holistic approach. I had always felt like I was separated from my knee and leg somehow—like they were problems that needed to be fixed with enough discipline.

Somehow I knew that I needed to "love my leg back to wellness," not beat it into submission.

And David was of the same mind, and I felt better right away.

"The energy in your knee is blocked," he told me.

"Yes, I know," I said. "What I don't know is why and how to unblock it."

I knew my leg was a "teacher" for me, and I knew that I needed to learn how to hear what it was trying to tell me. I had known that since our time at Lake Allatoona, but I apparently wasn't getting it.

My journals had already told me as much. They had also told me that my leg would guide me to better health if I could learn to listen to it.

I had ignored my body for years, and now my leg was "waking me up" to it once again. I couldn't ignore my leg and, therefore, I couldn't ignore my body any more either.

It's so easy to take your body for granted, isn't it? At least until it doesn't work anymore.

So my injured leg was helping me become conscious of my body once again. And it had also led me to David who, in addition to working with my injured knee area, was waking up my whole body through his massage work.

There were several sessions where I felt a deep emotional release as he massaged my body. It was clear to me that the physical massage was touching deeply buried emotions that I hadn't yet been able to excavate.

And I probably never would have found David if I hadn't needed additional help with my injured leg—so, yes, it was becoming clear that my leg was indeed my teacher, and was leading me in the direction of deeper healing.

Twenty-Five

Max and I slowly but surely put our life back together again, and in such a way that it was more fun filled and active than ever before.

Max had been trained as a therapy dog in 2005, but we really had only started doing a little therapy work before we had left on our RV trip in the spring of 2006. And, then, of course, we couldn't do it for several months after we returned because of my mobility limitations.

Therapy dogs provide a wonderful service, and, in my opinion, are great healers when they visit people in nursing homes, hospitals, and children in schools and libraries.

We had stumbled into therapy work by accident. Our friend Jane at PetSmart was a trainer and test administrator for Therapy Dogs International (TDI) and she had suggested that Max be trained as a therapy dog.

Since I had already seen what a healing affect he was having on me, I thought it would be a great idea to share him with other people. And I had read about dogs needing a sense of work and this seemed like a good type of work for my big, friendly dog.

Once we had completed the training and passed the test, we joined a group of people who regularly did therapy work with their dogs. This was great for us because it gave Max a chance to meet other very sociable and well-trained dogs while we were also able to learn the ropes of therapy work from them.

Max, of course, was a natural. This was one place where his size was an advantage since he was as tall as most hospital beds, and, therefore, people who were bed-ridden could still pet his head. He has very soft big ears and people just seemed to love to stroke them.

And Max seemed to know just what to do, and how to make people feel loved.

It was just so clear to me, once again, that animals can play such a healing role in our lives. And after every therapy visit, I felt more healed myself.

So as fall approached and my mobility became stronger, I realized that we needed to get back to our therapy work—for both of us.

We reconnected with our pet therapy group and joined them for a series of visits around Halloween. Max patiently wore a pumpkin suit on his back that I had fashioned from a child's costume that I had found at a thrift store.

All of the therapy dogs wore costumes, but most of them were little dogs. I didn't want Max to look out of place, so I had fashioned a costume for him as well. And he looked very cute in it and it didn't seem to bother him at all.

In fact, over time we have accumulated costumes for all of the major holidays, and Max wears them with great patience. He particularly likes his "holiday bell" collar since I had given him a lot of treats to help him get used to the sound. Now he always looks for the treat whenever I bring the bell collar out for him to wear.

As we became more active in pet therapy work, I began to realize that our best visits were when we returned to the same facility. Because Max was so big, some people were a little afraid of him until they had gotten to know him. It seemed that it might work better for us if we could find one or two facilities and go there on a regular basis.

So I began to look around for such a facility a little closer to home. We had been traveling all over the four county area with our pet therapy group, and it would be more convenient to find something closer.

And then in the mail I received a notice about hospice volunteer opportunities, and I thought that might be a good area for us to pursue. And, as it turned out, it was even better than I ever could have imagined. Because of Max, I was going to walk on a path that I had walked before—but now at a much deeper level.

I had been introduced to hospice work when I had gone out to Oregon in the fall of 2003 when my mother-in-law, Ina, was ill with cancer. Actually, she was my ex-mother-in-law but we were still very close, and she and the family had asked me to come out for a visit when she became so ill.

I was also close—and still am—to my former husband's sisters and brothers, and I wanted to give them support as well during this challenging time.

Back in 2003, I didn't know anything about the dying process, and, probably like most people, I didn't really want to know anything.

Death was frightening to me. I had been taught to fear death and to avoid anything to do with it.

But Ina was to teach me that death can be a very healing and transformative process.

Twenty-Six

When I flew out to Portland to be with Ina and her family, I was assuming that I would stay for a week or so and then fly home. We knew that she had cancer, but she had beaten it before and we assumed she would do the same thing again.

Ina lived with her daughter, Matilda, and her two sons, Wil and Charlie, also lived in the area. So she had her family around her, and they were giving her a lot of good loving care. They had lost Bill, her husband of fifty years, just a few months earlier after several months of illness, and she and the whole family were exhausted from that situation.

I didn't have Max at the time so I was free to fly out there and give them whatever help I could.

Ina's condition when I arrived seemed pretty good. She was as chipper as always, and I enjoyed spending time with her chatting about this and that. Matilda was working at the time, so I could help with Ina's care when she was gone at work.

However, it wasn't long before Ina's health began to decline, and decline pretty rapidly. She was admitted to the hospital and the doctor did not give her a good prognosis.

That was a difficult time. We had all expected her to recover. To tell a patient and her family that she probably won't recover is like getting socked in the stomach. You just can't believe that it is really happening, and you don't want to believe it.

Needless to say, we were all in shock and it was not easy to deal with.

Ina decided that she wanted to go home, and a hospital bed was brought out to the house so she would be more comfortable. Her daughter Kay Sue flew out to join the care-giving team, and her son Doug also came for a visit, but couldn't stay because of his work commitments. Her grandson, Aaron, and granddaughters, Molly and Jenny, were also with her as often as their work schedule would permit.

The next few days and weeks were pretty difficult. While she was surrounded by her loving family and never left alone, it was still a time of sadness as hope for her recovery continued to diminish.

I had agreed to stay and help the family with her care, but I had no idea what that would really involve.

What it turned out to mean—for me at least—was a complete change in my attitude about death and the dying process.

It is so unfortunate that our culture shrouds the death experience in so much fear. It is really such a natural part of our human experience, and one that I have come to treat with great reverence.

That was what Ina taught me. A true class act through it all, Ina went through the dying process with great dignity and grace. She truly became radiant in her final hours.

And the people from hospice were such a God-send. None of us really knew what to expect as she went further into the dying process, and that created a lot of fear and uncertainty in and of itself.

As soon as the hospice team arrived, they explained to us what was happening and how we could best help Ina at this time. That was a great relief to all of us, and enabled us to care for her much more effectively.

Ina passed away about two weeks later in a state of great peace. The family was there holding her hands at the time, and singing her favorite songs. I am sure that her spirit was singing right along with us as she passed on to the next world.

That was in the fall of 2003, and the experience had a profound impact on me. But it would take a couple of years before I could process it enough to be able to act on it.

It was also on the flight home from Oregon that I found that ad for the dog blanket that I had mentioned earlier. The dog in the ad looks exactly like Max, and he came into my life just a short six months later.

Every time I look at it I am reminded of the mystery and power of the divine universe.

Twenty-Seven

So when I got the notice about volunteering at the hospice center in early 2007, I knew right away that I needed to investigate it further. Max had led me there through our work in pet therapy, but it would really turn out to be a mission for me.

And the lessons that Ina had given me several years earlier were about to come into play and take me to a whole different level of consciousness.

There are many hospice organizations in our area, with the largest being the Hospice of the Western Reserve. It is one of the largest hospice programs in the country, and they have over 1200 volunteers. One of the interesting features of hospice programs is that they are highly committed to providing service through volunteers, and 10% of all their work is done by volunteers.

So I called and signed up for their volunteer training program which was to begin that spring. It was a six week program that would begin in late March and end in early May.

And again, my initial enthusiasm at the idea began to be clouded with resistance. "Did I really want to get into 'that type' of work? Six weeks was a big commitment of time—can I really afford to give it that much time? And what about taking another motorhome trip this spring—doing this training would rule that out."

I wrote about this resistance in my journals, and I was surprised by how strong it was. But I also knew in my gut that it was exactly what I needed to do.

So I did it.

I completed the training and became a full-fledged hospice volunteer that May. The training program was surprisingly extensive, and it gave me the opportunity to explore the issue of death and the dying process in much greater depth.

As I went through the training process, I realized that I no longer felt any fear about death or the dying process. My experience with Ina had given me a whole different perspective on death, and it had taught me to see it as a beautiful and natural part of our human experience.

I actually felt a sense of peace and wonder about the death experience. So I decided, in addition to our pet therapy work, to sign up to become a vigil volunteer.

As a vigil volunteer, you are asked to sit with a person as they experience the dying process and offer them whatever comfort and support that you can. Vigil volunteers are often called in by the hospice nurse when the family needs such support, or when a patient does not have any family with them at that time.

I have had the great privilege of being with several people as they pass on, and I can assure you that it is a beautiful experience.

It has also been my privilege to have supported a number of families as they went through the death experience with a relative. Several have written me thank you notes expressing their gratitude for my support at that time. My gift to them is to help them see the death experience for what it really is: a natural and final step on our journey through life.

These experiences have had and continue to have a profound impact on me, and have greatly deepened my spiritual beliefs. And I know that I have Ina and Max—and my angels—to thank for these inspiring lessons.

Twenty-Eight

Because of the hospice training, we hadn't been able to travel in the motorhome that spring, and I was itching to get back in it.

I had received a call in April informing me that I would need to move the motorhome out of the storage facility that it had been in all winter because they had sold the building.

So where was I going to put it?

There were several outdoor storage areas available, and I began to visit them to find the one that I wanted to use.

And during that process, the idea came to me that maybe I could find a place to plug in the electrical cord so I could have electricity in it while it was parked. I thought it might be fun to be able to use it even while it was parked during the summer.

And then I thought, why not park it in an actual RV campground over the summer where I could use it fully? Why put it in storage when I could actually use it?

This was an "inspired" idea and I give my angels full credit for the whole thing.

I can always tell when an idea is inspired: it has a lot of

energy attached to it. I get really excited about it and can't wait to get started on it. But it also often has an element of resistance attached to it that I have to work through as well.

As I mentioned earlier, I had experienced the same type of resistance with the idea of my becoming a hospice volunteer. The good news was that I was beginning to "witness" this in myself in such a way that I could handle the resistance more effectively. I wasn't doing a great job with it yet, but I was doing a better job.

And that was the case with this idea too. I couldn't wait to get in the car with Max and go looking for a good campground nearby—and hopefully one with a pond or near the Lake so Max would be able to go swimming often. But I also had to listen to my "voice of fear" tell me all the reasons why I shouldn't do it.

But again, the mantra *feel the fear and do it anyway* was with me and guiding me forward.

After looking at about twenty campgrounds in three different counties, we finally found Country Lakes Campground. It was about thirty minutes from the condo and had just about everything that we had been looking for—including a big fresh water pond in which dogs were allowed to swim.

And as I stood looking at the beautiful blue water of the pond, I just knew that Max was going to love it and that it was the right thing for me to do. So I signed us up for a seasonal site before I could change my mind, and we were set to get started.

Twenty-Nine

Harriet, one of the owners of the campground, took us around to look at the five or six sites that were still available for seasonal use, and I chose one that was up on a hill and that offered a view of one of the lakes.

The site needed a lot of work, however. There hadn't been a camper on it for a year or longer, and it had gotten fairly overgrown with weeds and other debris. But I could see that it had great potential, and it was reasonably close to the swimming pond for Max.

At one point, the resistance popped back up and I started second guessing myself again, wondering if I was really doing the right thing. "Can this site really be fixed up OK? It's going to take a lot of work. Am I sure that I'm up to this? Should I be spending all this money?"

But I knew that was just my "little voice of fear" still making noise in my head. I was learning, however, not to let it have as much "air time" since I had come to realize that I was much better off listening to my intuition and following its lead.

And, again, Max was helping to lead me forward—just the image of him enjoying going for a daily swim in the pond was enough to keep me motivated even in the face of the fear.

So I started thinking about what I was going to need to take out there and realized that I would need a lawn mower. I had given mine up when I had moved out of my house several years ago, and hadn't needed one in the condo since they had a lawn crew do the yard work.

But the universe didn't just bring me a lawn mower, it brought me all kinds of helpful items. And this, once again, just reinforced my belief that I was on the right path, and gave me more courage to stick to it. And it also put that little voice of resistance in its proper place—silent.

The first Friday I went out to look for a mower at garage

sales, I found the perfect one for $30—a Craftsman mulcher/mower with the large wheels in back.

I had owned several Sears Craftsman mowers over the thirty or so years of living in houses with large yards, and I had really had good luck with them. And to have the mulching feature was particularly nice since it would save me from bagging all the grass and reseed the lawn out there at the same time.

So I was pretty excited about that find. I paid for the mower and then made arrangements to come back and pick it up the next day since I had to go to a meeting that afternoon.

I also knew that it would be better to load it just once into the trunk of my car since it was a little heavy and awkward. And then I could take it directly to the campground, which I was going out to on Saturday.

When I went by to pick it up Saturday morning, there was a lovely patio umbrella sitting on the neighbor's tree lawn. It even matched the motorhome colors of blue and gray.

It was being left out for the trash and I asked the owner if it worked OK and if I could please have it. "It works great," she said, "we just got a new furniture set and don't need it anymore, and you're more than welcome to have it."

So I told her thank you and wrapped it in the tarp that I carry in the car. That protected it from the grease and dirt from the mower when I put it in the trunk.

On subsequent garage sale ventures, I found a nice little fire pit for $10, a couple of planters for $1 apiece, and several pieces of lawn equipment (a rake, shovel, etc.) at next to nothing.

So all in all, the universe was being very generous in bringing me exactly what I needed and pretty quickly as well.

Later that summer, I bought a small shed for $35 from one of my neighbors so we even ended up with a place to store the equipment over the winter.

So the decision to take a campsite at Country Lakes was proving to be a good one. And I, once again, thanked my angels for all that they had brought us, and also for the inspiration to do it in the first place. Max and the angels were proving to be a very good team indeed.

Thirty

It was very quiet and peaceful out at the campground during the week, which was when Max and I were usually there. I wanted the solitude to start some writing projects, and loved being in such an inspirational place.

I find nature, as I've said before, to be very healing and a good place to tap into creative energy. It was very nice to be away from the bustle of the city and just have the birds serenading us as we sat on our new little patio outside the motorhome.

A patio that my friend Bob and I built with paving stones that my neighbor was willing to sell quite inexpensively. We used the extra gravel that was already on the driveway as a foundation for the paving stones, and then filled in the cracks with sand.

It took us several days of hard, hot labor to do it, but the result was terrific. We even made a place for the propane barbeque grill that I had gotten free from my neighbor after he had bought a big new one.

Bob attached the big patio umbrella to the end of the picnic table that the campground provided so we had a nice shady place to eat our meals outdoors. We added a couple of bird feeders and a bird bath for our feathered friends and we were set to go.

All in all, we had turned it into a very comfortable and attractive campsite.

Several of our neighbors came over to complement our work and to tell us how much nicer the site looked than it had in the past.

We were very pleased with how everything had turned out, and loved being out there. I later realized that it was "our backyard" since we didn't have one at the condo, and I had really missed not having a yard for so many years. And Max just loved being outside every moment that he could be there.

And we were even able to entertain out there: my longtime friends, Jo Ann and Carolyn, came out for a weekend and we had a great time. They had never seen the motorhome and they were suitably impressed with its comfortable way of living. And they appreciated all the hard work that had gone into making such a nice patio and outside living area.

So with the campsite finished and Max enjoying his daily swims, it also became the perfect place for me to read and start some of the writing that I had wanted to do. And I got quite a bit done.

Most of what I was reading and journaling about had to do with the consciousness process—I was eager to learn whatever I could since it seemed so confusing at times.

While I felt that I was making progress on my own personal journey towards greater consciousness, I also felt that part of me was still resisting it.

I had hoped that someone could tell me what was involved

so that I could push through this remaining resistance.

There are a lot of good books out there about the process, and I felt like I must have read all of them all by that point. But I was still experiencing that feeling of having these terrific insights and then falling back into my old patterns of resistance.

I have come to conclude that our paths towards spiritual consciousness can often be marked by just such a pattern: moving forward and then falling back. Experiencing a break-through and then suffering a set-back. It is that "chutes and ladders" process that I described in the first part of the book.

So that summer was a period of my continuing to climb that mountain of greater conscious awareness, but also still experiencing periods of doubt and resistance.

The good news for me was that I could tell that the periods of time when I felt I was in the present moment were expanding. I could live in that state for longer stretches of time, and the periods of doubt were shorter.

While the periods of resistance were shorter, they also seemed more intense. But my faith was growing stronger too, and I was able to handle these "rough waters" even though they were very challenging at times.

In reviewing my journals from that summer, I can see that this process was happening on a regular basis. I have come to believe that my growth in this area was the reason that the divine had led me to that lovely campground in the first place.

In that peaceful and spiritual place, I could go deeper into myself and excavate at an even deeper level. I felt like I was a butterfly struggling to break free of its cocoon—and it was taking a lot of thrashing around to crack it open.

Did my summer at Country Lakes allow me to finally break-through and know that I could live with presence all the time? To finally break free of the cocoon and fly free?

No. Unfortunately not completely.

But my faith was becoming stronger every day and I know that my time there helped me make significant progress in my personal commitment to living a more conscious life.

And Max had a great time out there, and particularly enjoyed his swimming time. He loved to retrieve the balls or the plastic frisbees that I would toss into the water. He always walked home well exercised and would sleep the rest of the afternoon away on our quiet and cool patio.

Thirty-One

One of my hopes for our summer at Country Lakes was to review my latest journals and put some of the insights that I felt I had been given down on paper so other people could benefit from them as well. I was beginning to envision putting them in the form of a book, but that seemed pretty challenging.

You may remember that I had started that process on our motorhome trip in 2005, and I had actually made some progress with the project while we were at Myrtle Beach.

But once we got back to Mentor after that trip, I didn't continue with the project for some reason. The press of daily life just once again took over I guess, and I never found the "window of time" in which to do it again.

I did get some of it done while we were out at Country Lakes, but it turned out to be a bigger job than I had anticipated.

So as I packed up the campsite and made it ready for winter, I made another promise to myself and the divine that this year I would get it done.

No more excuses and no more procrastination.

One of the insights that I had received out at Country Lakes was that I was still afraid to write the book I had been thinking about, and that this fear was just as much a part of the reason why the book had never happened as the time issue.

So what was I so afraid of, I asked myself.

I had a lot of trouble getting to the bottom of that question, but finally it came to me: to write such a book would require me to be willing to "expose my vulnerability" to the world.

It was one thing to write in my journals every day and put whatever thoughts came into my head down on the tablet. But it would be quite another thing to publish them for the entire world to see.

And a big part of my fear around the project was that I knew that I would have to be honest enough to share both my growth and my resistance (which displayed itself in pretty ugly behavior at times) if my book was going to be as effective as I hoped it would be.

And exposing myself that way was scary, and not exactly an easy thing to do.

You may have noticed in our society how common it is to want to only show the "perfect" parts of ourselves, and to try and hide the parts that we consider less than ideal.

So you can probably understand my dilemma: share the truth and be embarrassed, or hide it and feel inauthentic. So you can also probably understand why it took me so long to get it done.

I had to reach a place within myself where it was more

important to provide the information as a service to others than it was to look good to the world. It required me to tame my ego to the point where it was smaller than my spirit.

And it has taken me every moment of every day for many years to reach that point—and a lot of hard excavating work to boot. And the unconditional love that Max brought into my life was a big part of that process, and continues to be so.

But I finally got there—with my ego kicking and screaming at times—because the purpose that the book might serve finally became more important than my need to protect my "perfect" image of myself.

But even having reached that understanding and having made the commitment to write the book, I still wasn't able to get it done in Mentor. I just couldn't seem to focus there.

I had to make another motorhome trip with Max and this time we headed straight to Florida and our friends at the Quail Roost RV Campground, where you will remember we had stayed during my broken leg incident in 2006.

And this is the story of that important trip.

Thirty-Two

Max and I left Mentor in the motorhome on January 10, 2008, and were headed south to pay Bob a visit in Florida.

About thirty minutes into the trip, I started hearing a knocking sound up on the roof. I pulled off the highway and turned into a Honda dealership so we could stop in their big parking lot and check out the situation.

It was a Sunday and they were closed at the time.

Upon inspection, it looked like my TV antenna had come

loose from its slot up on the roof, and was knocking around in the strong winds that were beginning to blow.

"Rats," I said, "thirty minutes into our drive and we may be benched."

This trip, like our trip in 2005, had taken a lot of preparation, and Max and I were both eager to get out of town before more winter arrived. And getting even this far hadn't been that easy.

When I had gone to prepare the motorhome for the trip a few days earlier, I noticed that a small fishing boat was still parked near the front of the garage door where the motorhome was stored. I knew I wouldn't have enough room to back it out with the boat there.

I had talked with Kathy, the very nice manager of the storage facility, weeks earlier when someone had first parked the boat there.

They had originally assured me that they would leave that space empty when I had signed up to put the motorhome in the garage unit. I knew it would be a problem if anything was parked there because I had needed to cross through that parking space to get the motorhome in the garage unit in the first place.

I had not been able to winterize the motorhome due to a broken by-pass valve, and had been quite worried about my water lines freezing before I could get out of town. After driving around looking for some place else to park it, "angel" Kathy had offered to let us park it in the garage unit for a very reasonable fee.

So now I was in a sort of tricky situation: the motorhome was in the garage unit and the fishing boat was blocking me from getting out, and the men that Kathy had asked to move the boat hadn't done it.

Once again, I was at that "now what angels?" cross-roads.

As my departure day grew near, I began to wonder if I was even going to be able to leave. And if I didn't leave on that Sunday, I probably wasn't going to be able to leave for a week or better because another storm was due in later that day.

"So now what?" I thought to myself as Max and I sat in the car on Saturday afternoon staring at the boat.

"Maybe I could move it myself?" So I got out of the car and into the cold wind to look the situation over.

"Nope," I told Max when I got back in the car. "It's going to take more than me to move that thing."

I am very blessed with wonderful neighbors, and I realized that I needed to ask them to come to my aid. So I called my neighbor, Sam, and asked him if he and his son, Tom, could give me a hand.

Sam, of course, said yes, and that they would meet me at the storage facility at 8:30 am the next day. I had actually been planning on leaving later in the day to make sure the roads were good and dry. But they had plans to work that day, and it would be best for them to help me in the morning.

I had also made arrangements with my other neighbor, Marilyn, to drive Max and me—and our final bags of stuff—to the motorhome so I could leave my car in my garage.

Marilyn "does not do mornings" so I thought that might be a problem, but she—being the good sport that she is—said she would be happy to help us out.

So we all drove over to the storage facility early Sunday morning, and Sam and Tom moved the boat. I hadn't noticed that the trailer it was on had a flat tire, so that made moving it all the harder.

But they got it out of my way, I backed up the motorhome, and then they put the boat back in its original spot—or as close as they could get given its weight and the flat tire.

They took off to go to their painting job, and Marilyn and I unloaded her car with my bags of stuff—like the food and other perishables that have to be loaded at the last minute.

After a little ball chasing time for Max to get him ready to travel, we were all set to hit the road. And it was only about 10 am—2 hours ahead of schedule.

After stopping to get fresh gas and recheck the air in the tires—I had learned that lesson and wasn't about to forget it—we headed west on I-90 to pick up I-71 south and begin our drive to Florida. Being January, I knew any place further north wouldn't be warm enough, so we were heading straight to Florida.

Thirty-Three

But not with a broken antenna flapping around on the roof.

Motorhome antennas are fairly large and ungainly pieces of equipment. Being an older motorhome, mine was particularly large and ungainly.

"So now what?" I thought to myself.

Maybe I could climb up on the roof and tie it down?

While I had mastered driving and using the systems of the motorhome pretty well over the preceding three years of traveling in it, being up on the roof was not appealing.

Nor was climbing up the ladder attached to the motorhome with my still sore left leg.

It had been sunny when we were at the storage facility, but now the storm clouds and cold wind had taken over making the whole situation even bleaker.

"OK angels, what now?" I asked the air.

And up walked a young man who asked me if I had a problem.

I explained the situation and, sure enough, he volunteered to climb up on the roof and tie the antenna down for me.

Thrilled to pieces, I quickly got some rope from one of the storage compartments—silently thanking Bob for putting it there years earlier—and tossed it up to him. He had climbed up to check out the situation to see if he could detach the antenna rather than tie it down.

But it couldn't be detached, so he used the rope to secure it as best as he could.

I thanked him profusely and gave him some money for his assistance. It turned out that he lived across the street and also worked at the Honda dealership. He had seen me turn in and had come over to see if I needed anything.

How nice is that?

"Good work, angels—two points for you guys."

And, yes, I talk to my angels all the time now. Call me crazy, but I do it any way and it seems to work out just fine.

Thirty-Four

So now it's close to noon and the storm is making its presence known.

"Better hit the road," I said to Max, "and hit it quick."

I'm sure you're thinking that this sounds a lot like our trip in 2005, and you'd be right. There are just a lot of things that can happen when you are traveling in a big, and now older, motorhome.

But we always seem to muddle through with the help of a lot of good people and a busy crew of angels.

After our successful first journey in the motorhome in 2005, Max and I had become confirmed RV travelers. Our initial reasons for choosing to travel in the motorhome had proven to be correct: we loved the space and comfort it provided, and the freedom of going wherever and whenever we wanted.

And I had, over the last several years, learned how to operate all of the systems on the motorhome so we traveled in "high comfort" most of the time, depending upon the weather.

Motorhomes are like tin cans—they are very reflective of the weather conditions. They can get very hot in warm weather and very cold in cold weather, so there are times when the temperature is not quite ideal, even with two air conditioners and a furnace.

And you will remember that some of our earlier trips in the motorhome were not so comfortable because I didn't really understand the systems, and we ended up leaving when the weather was awfully cold at night.

And, yes, we were headed south on I-71 again and expected to make it as far as the greater Cincinnati area once again.

Thirty-Five

Once the antenna was secured the best that it could be, we

resumed our trip and made pretty steady progress for the next several hours.

We stopped at a rest stop north of Columbus for a snack and a walk around the park for Max. We had gotten the whole "travel mindfully" approach in place, so it was a nice, slow, steady drive. And, oddly enough, driving this way we actually made better time than on our other trips.

Because all the RV campgrounds in the area were still closed for winter, I had decided to camp over night in a Wal-Mart parking lot. I had picked one out at our last rest stop. I now travel with an atlas that lists all of the store locations—something I really needed on my trip in 2005.

So our first night was spent in Florence, Kentucky, which was about 30 miles south of Cincinnati.

While we were both somewhat tired from the drive, we weren't worn out. And I felt a sense of peace and contentment as I realized that I was making progress in listening to my inner wisdom. I had learned my lesson about pacing myself so we enjoyed the trip instead of traveling unconsciously and getting exhausted.

Max and I took a nice long walk around the area and he seemed to enjoy all the new sights and smells. Walking Max always brings me back to the present moment and helps me appreciate the simple things in life.

Once I had fed him supper, I walked across the street and ordered some takeout food from a Chinese restaurant. I felt fortunate that they were open on a Sunday night, although it seemed like I was their only customer at the moment.

While I was waiting for the food to be prepared, I chatted with the hostess and she asked where we were from. I explained about our trip south to get into warmer weather, and that I was traveling with my dog, Max, in the motorhome across the street.

"By yourself?" she exclaimed.

"Just me and my dog," I answered, and this time I wasn't at all hesitant to say it.

That reminded me how my attitude had matured; I no longer felt a bit embarrassed to be traveling with only Max.

"My dog is a big Lab and he's very good company. We have a great time together," I elaborated.

The hostess laughed and pointed out the motorhome to the waitress as she came out with my food.

As I walked back to the motorhome, I looked up at the bright stars shining in the heavens, and I laughed with the universe: "we've come a long way since that first 'knee-knocking' trip a few years ago haven't we. Thank you for all your patience, guidance and support. Now it is such fun!"

Thirty-Six

We were off bright and early the next day. With the traffic light and the roads dry, we were able to make good time without feeling rushed. I knew that it would be wise to get as far south as possible that day because a cold front was coming right behind me.

I was a little chagrined to be trying to "out-run" the weather again, but I knew that I had made the right choice in staying home over the last couple of months, and that I would do it again if need be.

I had planned on leaving in the fall—right after Thanksgiving—until my old apartment complex had a fire on October 23rd that destroyed the building and affected one of my friends and former neighbors, Jay Robert Klein.

Jay Robert had lived across the hall from me in the Village Green apartments, and we had grown close over the years. He had a little Corgi dog named Patty, and we would often visit when he was out walking her. And one of our other neighbors, Sandy, was a good friend of Jay Robert's and we would often get together for dinner or a chat in one of our apartments.

When I adopted Max and had to move out of the building, I had left my piano behind for Jay Robert to use since I wouldn't have room for it in the smaller condo in Mentor. I thought it would be a shame to put a fine musical instrument in storage when he could be enjoying it.

I was really shocked when Jay Robert called to tell me about the fire. It was the second building in the eleven building complex to be destroyed by fire and water damage in the last few years.

Another building had been destroyed by fire and water damage in February of 2004. I had actually considered moving after that fire, and then adopting Max that May made it a necessity. And, here three years later, our apartment building was destroyed by a very similar fire.

So if it hadn't been for Max, I might very well have still been there and would have lost all of my possessions as well. Not that I think possessions are all that important, but it would have been a dangerous and scary ordeal in any case.

And it certainly affected my friend, Jay Robert, who had turned 90 years old that August.

While he was normally very active, he had fallen a few months earlier and had injured his knee. So he was actually using a wheelchair and a walker to get around when the fire occurred.

Fortunately, he made it out of the building even though he had to use the stairs. Unfortunately, he also took another fall when the wheelchair went out from under him as he was rushing to leave. So he made it out alive, but had injured his knee again pretty severely.

About a week after the fire, the tenants were allowed back into the building to review the damage and claim whatever they could of their possessions. But with the elevator not working and his knee injury, Jay Robert couldn't get into his second-floor apartment to tell the salvage people what he wanted to reclaim.

Once he told me that, I offered to go and do it for him. It was a real mess—they had put the equivalent of ten Olympic-size swimming pools of water on the building and there was a lot of damage as a result. But by talking with him on my cell phone, we were able to go through the mess as best as we could and identify what he wanted the salvage people to take that they hadn't already, which was quite a bit.

The insurance adjuster and salvage contractor seemed to think that they just needed to itemize all his possessions and write him a check. Apparently, they just weren't listening to him when he said he wanted his own things, not new furniture.

So he asked me to intervene again and I was able to work it out so that he got most of his wooden furniture repaired and returned. The sofas and other fabric pieces were lost because of the risk of mold from the water damage, along with most of his personal papers. But we were able to reclaim most of his art and many of his other personal possessions.

We were able to slowly get his new apartment to feel like home again when his things were returned. And,

Mary, his housekeeper of many years, did a wonderful job of unpacking all the boxes and putting the apartment together for him again.

And I do mean slowly—it took two full months for this process to work itself out, and I'm sure it would have taken a lot longer if he had been trying to do it all by himself. It took me making a lot of phone calls to keep the ball rolling—nothing seemed to happen if they didn't get nagged a bit.

Going through a fire like that—and being injured again in the process—had been quite an ordeal for Jay Robert. I am sure that losing so many important personal possessions in a fire would be hard for anyone, but at 90 years of age, it had to be particularly difficult.

But as things started coming back together, he started feeling better too. And, while I'm sure that the whole experience will always be a bad memory for him, he was slowly able to put his life together again and get back on his feet.

Unfortunately, my piano didn't fare as well—it was a total loss. It had been destroyed by the water, not the fire, but it was still ruined. But with Jay Robert's help, his insurance company reimbursed me for the piano, although that also took a lot of work. While it was a shame to lose the piano, I would still rather have had him be able to enjoy it for those three or so years than to have put it in storage.

Some people were surprised that I was willing to spend so much time to help Jay Robert like I did, and my only thought was, "why wouldn't I?"

What could ever be more important in life than extending a hand to a friend in need? I believe that it's often the simple and most basic kindnesses in life that ultimately mean the most.

The fire, while a tragedy and an ordeal, had the "hidden" blessing of bringing Jay Robert and me closer than we had been before it happened. I had missed seeing him after Max and I moved to Mentor, and the fire gave us a reason to be back in frequent contact. He is a friend that I treasure and am blessed to have him in my life.

So, in that way, the fire was also a gift.

Thirty-Seven

So that was why we were now out-running another snow storm. But, as I mentioned earlier, we made good time on our second day of travel. We went from the Wal-Mart parking lot in Florence, Kentucky to a nice RV campground a little south of Atlanta. And this time we were able to get around Atlanta fairly easily, which I also considered a blessing.

We had made such good time driving the day before that I decided we could stay there for an extra day and get the motorhome better organized. We were also out of the freeze zone so I could hook up the water lines and clean the motorhome properly. And we now had electricity and a sewer hook-up as well.

Max and I had met a friendly dog and its owner on our morning walk, and the two dogs had a great time chasing each other in the big open field. I know that Max enjoyed the romp after two days of traveling and only getting a few walks along the way. There really is nothing like a good chase to run out all that extra energy in a dog.

We got back on the highway the next morning, headed to Florida. I wasn't trying to get all the way to Quail Roost that day since I knew that I couldn't make it before dark. I wanted to get there when it was daylight to make it easier for us to get parked and settled once we arrived.

So the fourth night found us in a campground south of Gainesville, Florida, with a three to four hour drive left to get to Quail Roost the next day.

Since we had a little extra time that next morning, we stopped at a Wal-Mart along the way and got some groceries and other things that we would need for our stay. I had cleaned the refrigerator the day before so it was now ready to get stocked with milk and other necessities.

We arrived at Quail Roost about 2 pm that day, and the weather was in the low 70's.

"Now this is more like it," I said to Max as we pulled in and parked at the office.

Nancy, one of the owners of the campground, came out to greet us. I had taken Max out to stretch his legs and he gave her a big hello as well—and then proceeded to "water" one of her new bushes while my back was turned to give Nancy a hug.

"Great way to make a good impression," I told him as I apologized to her. I wished that I had thought to make a stop and take him out just before we had gotten to the campground, but it hadn't occurred to me.

The incident was particularly embarrassing since Randy and Nancy, the owners of the Quail Roost Campground, had a no dogs policy for long-term campers. They had been nice enough to make an exception to allow us to come and spend time again with Bob.

They had made the same exception when we had stayed there in 2006 with my broken leg situation—so I really felt very grateful to them and the last thing I wanted was for Max or me to cause them any trouble.

So we start off with him peeing on her new bush.

But she seemed to take it in stride. I did keep my eye on that bush the whole time I was there and was going to replace it if it showed any signs of not doing well. But it seemed to be OK, fortunately.

Thirty-Eight

We arrived on January 14th and left on April 6th—almost 3 months later.

I hadn't planned on staying anywhere near that long, but both Max and I were having a great time and the weather up north just kept on being winter. Every time I thought about leaving, the weather would turn bad up north and discourage me from setting out.

Apparently, the universe wanted us to stay right where we were—and to enjoy ourselves while we were there. And it was easy to become part of the campground community—the owners and campers were so nice and friendly that we felt right at home.

Bob—also known as Roberto in the campground—was still part of the work crew at Quail Roost and would spend his mornings on maintenance projects on the grounds. Randy and Nancy had also opened a new retail RV business across the street from the campground, so the guys were busy helping to get that operation up and running as well.

I wanted to make a contribution to the campground as well, so I would help Nancy with the country line-dancing class that was held every Thursday morning. The women in the class were all very good dancers so it was fun to help them with a few new dances that I had learned up north.

Bob and I enjoyed several dance events at both the Moose and Elk Lodges over that three-month period. They had special dances for all the holidays, including Valentine's

Day, St. Patrick's Day, Easter, and several other special dances including a Charity Ball and a Luau.

Bob and I had actually met dancing at Springvale dance club in the Cleveland area back in the spring of 1995—a long time ago. Over the years, we had continued to dance together and always seemed to have a very good time.

We both enjoy learning new dances and placed a high priority on dancing well—and often spent extra time practicing to be able to do it "just right." Bob is a very good dancer, and I have always felt very fortunate to have him as a partner.

We also liked to listen to karaoke at the Elks almost every Tuesday night, and often at the Moose Lodge on Saturday nights. We would also go to one or the other on Friday nights to dance to a local band.

And that is why I had to give karaoke a try on my own, as I described in the beginning of this section. I was determined to give it a try before I headed back north, and just hoped that I would have the courage to finally do it some night.

So one Saturday night at the Moose, even though I was scared to death, I finally said to Bob, "I'm tired of being a chicken," and got up and put my name in the hopper. But I got even more nervous as I waited to be called.

I knew that I had to do it—or at least to try. Once I said to myself that I wanted to do it, and then said that I was too scared to do it, I knew that my lot was cast—I had to face my fear and do it.

Fear is a funny thing. It seems to get bigger the more you think about it.

And as I sat there that night, I just knew that I would be

so disappointed in myself if I let that opportunity go by, and, in essence, let fear win.

Bob was very supportive and said to me, "if you can drive a 33 foot motorhome all over the country by yourself, you can do this, I know you can."

All I could think of was that nobody was watching me do that like they were going to watch me do this.

So finally the DJ calls out, "James, is there a James in the house?"

And I just knew that he meant me.

After he loudly called "James" a few more times and no one else stood up, I realized that I was going to have to stand up and ask him if he meant "Janet."

Just add a little more embarrassment to the picture why don't you, I thought to myself.

But I stood up, walked down the aisle, and belted out "Eighteen Wheels and a Dozen Roses," a song made popular by Kathy Mathia in the late 1990's.

It wasn't a great song for my voice, but it was one of the few that I recognized off of the list that the DJ had available on the karaoke machine.

Bob and our friends said that I did great—but I know that they were just being nice to me. I was nervous—and my voice was nervous—so it couldn't have been that great, but I did do it.

That was all that was really important—I didn't let fear win—I conquered my fear and got up there and sang karaoke for the first time ever.

And it wasn't so bad—I can see why people like to perform—I definitely felt a little thrill while I was up there.

And I know that the next time will be a lot easier.

So with all the dancing, karaoke singing, and playtime for Max, you can see why we didn't want to leave. Why leave all this fun and sunshine to go home to snow?

And I was finally writing the book.

Thirty-Nine

Yes, I wrote this book while staying at Quail Roost that winter—although it didn't feel like winter in 70 to 80 degree sunshine.

As I mentioned earlier, writing the book was something that I had wanted to do for years, but I just hadn't found the time and courage to do it.

And now I was able to do it—not without facing a lot of remaining demons—which came out as distractions. I was very good at finding lots of other things to do at the campground.

But I was finally in a physical space and an emotional place where I really felt like I could do it—or at least give it a good try.

I was beginning to realize that I didn't have all the time in the world ahead of me anymore, and what if something happened to me and I never got a chance to do it?

I remembered hearing somewhere that it is very sad if "someone dies with their song still in their heart" and I knew that I had yet to "sing my song."

Maybe the universe has a really good sense of humor and that is why it also brought me the challenge of singing karaoke—to help me get my "song" out.

So I was able to finally knuckle down and get to work on the book.

I would work on the book in the mornings while Bob was busy with his campground duties, and Max supported the process by keeping me company while napping on the sofa.

And Max and I always took a mid-morning walk to get some air and give him some more exercise chasing after his frisbees or tennis balls.

And the book really wrote itself. I typed the words, but the thoughts really just flowed through me. I believe that all creative work comes from the divine universe and this was no exception.

So you can really consider this book a gift from the universe to you.

As I sit here in the motorhome and type these final words, I feel very grateful to the divine universe for the journey that it has "unfolded" for me.

Writing the book required me to relive all of these experiences and the lessons they taught me became so much clearer. As a result, I feel even more grateful and appreciative to the divine universe for this journey.

And I feel very grateful that it brought my children, Jennifer and William, into my life, Max into my life, Bob into my life, my family and friends into my life, and all the other wonderful people who have played such an important role in my life journey.

And I am equally appreciative of all the people and experiences that may have appeared "negative" at the time: I know that they all played an equally important role in teaching me what the universe had in mind for me to learn.

I accept what has been and what is currently in my life—totally and completely. And I accept it with peace and gratitude.

And Max and I wish the same for you. Happy travels.

*I am not afraid of storms because
I am learning to steer my ship.*

Louisa May Alcott

Epilogue

It is now September 22, 2008, which is the Autumnal (Fall) Equinox, and the book is finally ready to be launched. And it is only fitting that it be launched now, along with the Autumnal Equinox, since—at age 58—it represents the fall season of my life and the harvesting of much of my life experience.

And the Equinox is such an important time of year for me that it feels very appropriate to be bringing the book to the world at this time. The Equinox is important to me because—as you already know—it is the time of the year when the length of the day and night are equal or in harmony. And my entire intention with the book is to enhance harmony on the planet so what could be more perfect.

This perfect timing is the work of the divine universe, not me.

In my own human imperfection, I had felt a need to rush forward and get it printed as quickly as possible when I got back to Mentor in April. But then a wondrous thing happened—I realized that I needed to let go of the illusion of control and just let the process unfold with its own divine timing, and that my task was to go with that flow and just pay attention to what the universe wanted me to learn.

And I had a lot yet to learn.

As you know from the book, my life journey has been marked by the need to heal my wounds and face my fears in order to move forward and live a more conscious life. And by a conscious life I mean one where I am secure enough in my inner self that I can allow the divine to guide me and, by so doing, co-create a more loving, grateful, and peaceful existence for myself.

And a conscious life is a wonderful place to live. It is a little like moving to a new city—everything is fresh and new and exciting. And you have to find your way around this new place and it takes a little time to feel settled and comfortable. It also requires patience with yourself as you make a few wrong turns, but you learn from your mistakes and make the right turn the next time.

That clearly has been my experience—the chutes and ladders aspect of the process of becoming more conscious. Forward, backward, forward, backward—but always making a little more progress along the way, until finally you reach a summit and know that your life has changed forever. There may be more than one summit—there certainly was for me—but you are still making progress every step of the way.

At this time in our evolutionary history, the concept of living a conscious life is talked about but is not yet the mainstream way of thinking. So it will take courage to walk this path and stick to it when you are surrounded by people who still think very differently.

But I would hope that this book will encourage those of you who are on this path to keep going, and open a window to others who are just starting to consider this new way of being.

I do believe that it is our evolutionary destiny because it is the truth, and because it empowers all of us as individuals to be the best person that we can be. And, collectively, it empowers us to heal the world—which we obviously have a very real need to do.

And while I would certainly love to see more collective

action to heal the planet, I would not want us to underestimate the power and impact of our individual commitment to peace and healing. If each of us became just a little more loving towards ourselves and others, we would experience a very different world.

Each of us has a unique journey, and we hope that by sharing our journey that you will feel more empowered on your own life path.

I believe that we are all on our own unique paths towards consciousness—whether we know it or not. And I believe that becoming a more conscious person is what we are here to do—it is the natural evolution of our species.

As time goes on, I also believe that this "work" that we are all engaged in will become more acceptable in the mainstream and a natural part of our understanding of ourselves and others.

There are many avenues through which our consciousness can be expanded. In my own journey, certainly taking the time and making the sometimes painful effort to examine and heal my personal wounds and see the lessons in those experiences has been important. Spending time in nature and letting its presence heal me has also played a key role. Facing my fears with courage and perseverance has certainly been important to me, particularly in the last several years as shared in this story.

But certainly the most obvious and perhaps most dramatic catalyst in my life journey has been Max. Ever since he came into my life, I have been head over heels in love with him and, because of that love, determined to meet the challenges that he brought into my life. And, as you just read, he brought me quite a few—and big ones at that.

Max has taught me a great deal, including:

He taught me how to slow down enough to be present in my everyday life. I am reminded of that every day on our morning and evening walks.

He taught me to honor my body and my mobility with the broken leg experience. That experience also taught me patience and endurance—in great measure.

He taught me to appreciate and love nature—and to relax into it—in a way that I never fully understood before. He is so present with nature that I learn just by watching him.

He taught me to have confidence in myself and my abilities, and that I could indeed handle a big dog, a big motorhome and any other big challenges that come into my life.

He showed me how to love unconditionally, and taught me how to do it as well. He helped me learn to love myself—and that I didn't need to be perfect in order to be lovable.

He taught me how to be present in the now, in every moment of every day. He still does it much better than I do, but I'm learning more all the time by watching him do it.

And I'm sure that there are many more items to put on the list, and that the list will continue to grow in the years ahead.

I just feel very grateful and very blessed to have Max in my life, and very appreciative of all that he has taught me and is continuing to teach me. I know that he serves as an instrument of the divine, and that they couldn't have given me a better teacher.

And I know that I have changed from all of these experiences, and that my view of reality has shifted in fairly dramatic ways. This is what I now believe:

I see the world very differently than I did a few years ago; namely, I believe in the divine universe, and in the power of divine energy as love to heal ourselves and our planet.

I believe we are all connected through one divine energy field and that we can communicate with each other and "influence" each other (both positively and negatively) through that divine energy field.

I believe we need to watch and manage our thoughts at all times and live with as much positive presence as possible; and to learn to allow the divine to guide us in our daily thoughts and actions.

I believe that our purpose in life is to learn to live through this new perspective in order to bring service and healing to ourselves, to other people, to animals, and to everything else on our planet.

I believe that by living a life of joyful service that each of us can bring light to our little corner of the world and that is important in and of itself.

These beliefs have emerged from my life experiences— many of which I have shared with you in this book. I believe that our experiences in life are our most powerful teachers if we just understand them as such.

And I am happy to report that I have listened and learned from all of the experiences, and they have made it possible for me to "put my closet back in order." The mess on the floor that I couldn't see how to organize earlier in the book has been straightened out and neatly put away.

Keeping it that way will, of course, be an ongoing process, but that's life. We will constantly be receiving new things in our life that need to be sorted through. That keeps our life fresh.

And everyone has to learn to do this for themselves.
And I have confidence that we can all learn to do it, and
do it well.

No one will ever know you better than you know yourself.
Other people might be able to support you and encourage
you, but they can never replace that powerful inner
knowing that is yours alone.

So please listen to and honor that inner wisdom—it is your
key to learning to truly love yourself and everyone and
everything in your world.

And that, my friend, is the path to inner peace.

May peace be with you.

Let me be the flute through which God's breath flows.

Rumi

Acknowledgements

This book was indeed the work of many minds and many spirits, and I thank each and every one of you. Your contributions made it so much better than I ever could have made it alone.

I would also like to acknowledge and thank my family for all of their support. My children, Jennifer Eadie and her partner, Jef Green, and William Eadie, and his fiancée Christine Zuniga. My sisters and their husbands, Barbara and Frank Peterson, Linda and Don McNeill, and Nancy Barclay Moore. And also my former husband, Doug Eadie and his entire family. And in memoriam, my parents, Hope and George Bennett, my former in-laws, Ina and Bill Eadie, and my dear friend, Jay Robert Klein.

And a special thank you to my many friends and neighbors who are too numerous to name. Just know how much I appreciate you being a part of my life and letting me tend to your gardens. And to my longtime friends, thank you for being so supportive when I was going through the darkness; it is nice to be back in the light with you.

I would also like to thank two very special teachers in my life, Peace Pilgrim and Eckhart Tolle. Your words and actions have both guided me and inspired me on my own journey. And to my friends at the Institute for Noetic Sciences—your work has also been a real source of learning and inspiration, and I am proud to be a member.

And a special thank you to everyone at all the campgrounds we stayed at, particularly Quail Roost, Eagle Lake, Lake Allatoona, and Country Lakes—you have all been so wonderful and gracious to us.

And to my angels and the divine which is constantly guiding my life: thank you, thank you, thank you.

About the Author

Janet and Max on their trip to Myrtle Beach

Janet resides in Mentor, Ohio, with her yellow lab, Max. They enjoy doing pet therapy and traveling around the country in their motorhome. Janet also enjoys gardening, biking, and dancing. She has had an active professional career and has a doctorate from Case Weatherhead School of Management.

Visit www.travelswithmax.com for updates on their travels.

Max enjoying his first dog bed in his new home--the dog bed that fell on Janet's head.

Maureen, Steve, Rhymer, Seager, and Max enjoy some ball playing time at Eagle Lake Campground.

Janet and Max enjoy their patio at Myrtle Beach Campground.

Max retrieving two tennis balls at Eagle Lake.

Max pays Jay Robert a visit after the fire in his apartment which caused him to fall and injure his knee.

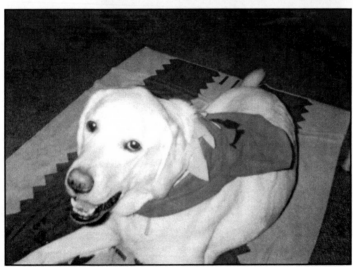

Max wearing his pumpkin costume for a therapy visit.

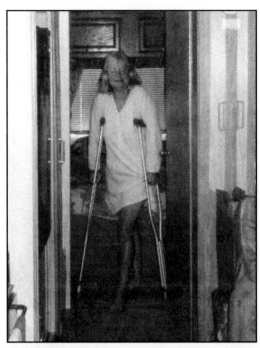

Janet on crutches in the motorhome after breaking her leg.

Janet journaling on the patio with Max at Quail Roost.

Bob and Max enjoy the campsite at Country Lakes Campground.

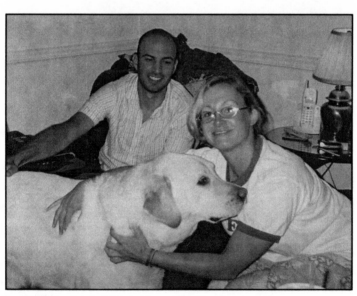

Jef and Jenny enjoy Max on their visit to Mentor to help Janet.

Janet's Florida "office" in the motorhome where she wrote the book.

Christine and Will with Mussie and Lucy.

Printed in the United Kingdom
by Lightning Source UK Ltd.
134868UK00001B/37/P